Color and Consciousness

Color
and
Consciousness

An Essay in Metaphysics

CHARLES LANDESMAN

Temple University Press

PHILADELPHIA

Temple University Press, Philadelphia 19122
Copyright © 1989 by Temple University. All rights reserved
Published 1989
Printed in the United States of America

The paper used in this publication meets the minimum
requirements of American National Standard for Information
Sciences—Permanence of Paper for Printed Library Materials,
ANSI Z39.48-1984

Library of Congress Cataloging-in-Publication Data
Landesman, Charles.
Color and consciousness: an essay in metaphysics / Charles Landesman.
p.   cm.
Bibliography: p.
Includes index.
ISBN 0-87722-616-4 (alk. paper)
1. Knowledge, Theory of.   2. Metaphysics.   3. Color (Philosophy).
4. Consciousness.   5. Perception (Philosophy).   6. Skepticism.   I. Title.
BD161.L32 1989
111'.1—dc19   88-29442
CIP

To
Arlyne, Erica, Jennifer and Steven, and Peter and Karen

Contents

Contents

Preface

The subject of this book is the status of secondary qualities, particularly colors. It attempts to establish a rather surprising conclusion, namely that nothing has any color. I call this conclusion *color skepticism,* and I try to defend it in the eighth and final chapter. I arrive at color skepticism as a result of discussing in Chapters One through Seven various philosophical accounts of the nature of color and finding them all wanting. Three accounts in particular are discussed in detail: first, that secondary qualities are dispositional properties of bodies; second, that they are physical microstates of bodies; and, third, that they reside in consciousness. These accounts share the assumption that any adequate theory must 'save' our common sense beliefs about secondary qualities. This means that an account is acceptable only if it implies that most of our ascriptions of secondary qualities are true. Color skepticism rejects that assumption. In the course of discussing the third view, which is called *subjectivism,* I am led, in Chapter Six, to make some remarks about the mind-body problem in general as well as to argue against the widely accepted view that perceptual experiences are representational or intentional.

One theme that runs through the course of this essay concerns the relation between science and common sense. I argue that scientific theory can justifiably lead us to revise our common sense view of the world and that the world as it is 'in itself', the world objectively viewed, is quite different from the world as it is 'for us'. Thus I cannot accept the view of Moore and Wittgenstein that our common sense beliefs and agreements constitute a rock bottom basis for human knowledge. Color skepticism is a stage in the unending process of human inquiry in developing an objective view of reality that abstracts from the illusion-producing peculiarities of the human cognitive apparatus.

Another theme that is discussed throughout concerns the structure of visual experience. I argue that experience is presentational rather than representational and that this is compatible with our perceptions' failure to be veridical to a large extent. I cannot pretend that the attempts I have made to resolve the puzzles that attend this view of experience are fully satisfactory, but a full discussion would require another book.

I have attempted to make this book self-contained so that it can be read with understanding by those who are not already instructed in the complexities of contemporary philosophy. It should be accessible to all those, no matter what their discipline, who have an interest in the philosophy of human knowledge. It can also be used by students of philosophy as an introduction to the problems it discusses.

I have indicated in the notes those individuals from whose writings and discussions I have learned the most. I have discussed the issues that I take up in this book for many years with Arthur

Collins. Although he will not agree with much of what is written here, the way it was written was influenced significantly by attempts to take account of his criticisms.

C. L.
July 7, 1988

Color and Consciousness

ONE

Introductory Remarks

In this essay, I intend to discuss certain aspects of the philosophical problem that is frequently described by the rubric "our knowledge of the external world." This is not really a single topic but a collection of interrelated issues that together constitute the problem of knowledge. One dominant strand of discussion in modern philosophy is Descartes's question: How can I know that there is an 'external' world? Given that an individual knower is directly acquainted only with his own experiences or with the ideas in his own mind, how can he validate his belief in the existence of other items such as bodies, other people, past events, gods, numbers, and so forth with which he is not directly acquainted but which are at best "represented" by his experiences and ideas? This is the problem of radical skepticism that Descartes formulated in his *Meditations* and that produced such fruitful philosophical reflections in the writings of Berkeley, Hume, and Kant.

Other philosophers, however, were not impressed by Descartes's radical skepticism. Hobbes and Locke, for example, although adopting a representational theory of knowledge, felt that the radical skepticism of Descartes was artificial and of no practical significance. They were impressed by the new scientific ideas that were emerging in their lifetimes. For Hobbes, the world consists of bodies in motion; the explanation for anything that happens, even an event in the human mind, must be formulated exclusively in the terms of this materialistic ontology. Although Locke was a dualist rather than a materialist, arguing that, in all probability, mind cannot be reduced to matter, he was impressed by the corpuscularian theory of matter that was being developed by his scientific friend Robert Boyle and others. The external non-mental world consists of corpuscles or atoms or clumps of them having size and shape, filling space, and capable of motion and rest. Locke calls these basic features of the corpuscles *primary qualities*.

Both Hobbes and Locke were more interested in making use of the new science for explanatory purposes than they were in doubting its truth. Neither was impressed by the anti-empiricist conclusions that Descartes's skepticism motivated. Both would have been repelled by the phenomenalistic and idealistic interpretations of science that Berkeley and Kant developed as alternatives to their own unhesitating realism.

One way in which they used the new science was to explain how human knowledge is possible. Human beings, after all, have bodies and are part of and are subject to the exigencies of the material world. Human knowledge begins with the impact of bodies upon the sense organs, which produce motions in the brain that cause objects to be sensed. A variety of conceptions or ideas can be generated from the data of sense, and these form the constitutents of the opinions and theories developed by the human mind. The mind is fundamentally a mechanism for extracting information from sense data. Whatever fails to get into the sense data via the sense organs and brain cannot become an object of knowledge.

This theory of knowledge is representational because the appearances or sense data or ideas of sensation represent the objects that cause them in virtue of containing information about them. Because of the way an object appears, I can tell that it is, for example, square. The information that it is square is, in some way, contained in the appearance. A direct non-representational theory would explain my coming to know that it is square by supposing that I am directly acquainted with the state of affairs of its being square. That it is square is something that is directly given to me; I *see* that it is square. Representational theories, however, challenge this common sense view on the grounds that it fails to fit in with our new understanding of how sense perception takes place: sensory appearances are mental items caused by a complex and strongly mediated series of events involving changes in the sense organs and brain. We are directly acquainted with the mental terminus of the series, not the external facts that initiate it. Common sense is misled here because of its ignorance of the causes of perception. Now that science has revealed the causes, direct realism must give way to representationalism. What we have directly and immediately are not the external facts that we claim to know, but signs of them.

In fact, Locke insists that the science of human knowledge should be called "*the Doctrine of Signs* . . . the business whereof, is to consider the Nature of Signs, the Mind makes use of for the understanding of Things, or conveying its Knowledge to others. For since the Things, the Mind contemplates, are none of them, besides it self, present to the Understanding, 'tis necessary that something else, as a Sign or Representation of the thing it considers, should be present to it. And these are *Ideas*."[1] Ideas are mental signs or representations of items that exist in nature. It is the ideas themselves, not the facts they signify, that are "present to the Understanding."

A representational theory of knowledge leads to a new set of problems. Once we have rid ourselves of the prejudices of common sense, particularly the view that we are directly acquainted with the objects and facts of the external world, we are no longer entitled to take for granted that how things appear accurately reflects how things really are. How things appear consists of a mental representation only indirectly and distantly related to how things are, the facts represented. It is at least possible that the organic and mental processes that produce the mental representations cause them to embody misinformation as well as information about the external world.

For the representational theories of early modern philosophy, the uncovering and explanation of error became just as important as accounting for knowledge. The view of Descartes, Hobbes, and Locke is that sense perception is a source of pervasive error about the true character of reality. This view is not original with them. It can be found earlier in the writings of Galileo. In speaking of heat in *The Assayer*, he writes:

> People in general have a concept of this [heat] which is very remote from the truth. For they believe that heat is a real phenomenon, or property, or quality, which actually resides in the material by which we feel ourselves warmed. Now I say that whenever I conceive any material or corporeal substance, I immediately feel the need to think of it as bounded and as having this or that shape, as being large or small in relation to other things, and in some specific place at any given time; as

being in motion or at rest; as touching or not touching some other body; and as being one in number, or few, or many. From these conditions I cannot separate such a substance by any stretch of my imagination. But that it must be white or red, bitter or sweet, noisy or silent, and of sweet or foul odor, my mind does not feel compelled to bring in as necessary accompaniments. Without the senses as our guides, reason or imagination unaided would probably never arrive at qualities like these. Hence I think that tastes, odors, colors, and so on are no more than mere names so far as the object in which we place them is concerned, and that they reside only in the consciousness. Hence if the living creature were removed, all these qualities would be wiped away and annihilated.[2]

Galileo makes the point that those features of bodies that Locke calls *primary qualities* are inseparable from them. The primary qualities are the necessary accompaniments of any imaginable material object. This view serves well to justify Galileo's celebrated claim that the language in which the book of nature is written is "the language of mathematics, and its characters are triangles, circles, and other geometric figures without which it is humanly impossible to understand a single word of it; without these, one wanders about in a dark labyrinth."[3] Geometry reveals the essential features of matter. The other features of bodies—colors, tastes, sounds, odors, and heat—those that Locke calls *secondary qualities,* "reside only in consciousness."

The secondary qualities, then, are properties in some way of our representations but not of the objects represented. With regard to the science of nature, they constitute noise rather than information. It is but a short step to draw the conclusion that our sensory representations are fundamentally erroneous and misleading. This is Hobbes's view when he speaks of "the great deception of sense":

> Whatsoever accidents or qualities our senses make us think there be in the world, they are not there, but are seemings and apparitions only. The things that really are in the world without us, are those motions by which the seemings are caused. And this is the great deception of sense.[4]

Hobbes offers a rather primitive explanation of why it is that we mistakenly 'project' secondary qualities upon bodies by suggesting that the motions in the brain caused by events in the eye "rebound" back into the optic nerve.[5] But his claim that the senses are deceptive, that though "the reall, and very object seem invested with the fancy it begets in us; Yet still the object is one thing, the image or fancy is another,"[6] does not depend upon the details of the explanation he offers.

Descartes bolstered his case for radical skepticism in the *Meditations* by pointing out the ways in which our senses are deceptive. Hobbes had no interest in taking Descartes's path. In his criticisms of the *Meditations*, Hobbes points out that the arguments for skepticism had been canvassed in ancient philosophy and that Descartes's arguments are unoriginal.[7] More important, he argues that the errors produced by our deceiving senses can be corrected by the senses. "For as sense telleth me, when I see directly, that the colour seemeth to be in the object; so also sense telleth me, when I see by reflection, that colour is not in the object."[8] Hobbes thus claims that, on the basis of evidence drawn from our deceptive senses, we can develop a correct theory of nature that allows us to identify the deceptions and to correct them. This is an important claim, but Hobbes does little to support it. In any case, Hobbes does not find it necessary to adopt Descartes's rationalism and theism in order to cure radical skepticism. He is not smitten by the illness and so has no need of the medicine.

One little-noticed feature of Hobbes's rejection of common sense realism about secondary qualities is that it is based upon his nominalism, his rejection of the reality of abstract entities such as species and genera. If colors are universals, then we can understand how the very color that is exhibited in the sense data can also be exemplified by the body in which we see it. But "the introduction of species visible and intelligible . . . passing to and fro from the object, is worse than any paradox, as being a plain impossibility."[9] The Aristotelian doctrine of sensible and intelligible species is considered by Hobbes to be a case of "insignificant Speech."[10]

Let us be clear about the nature of the deception that, according to both Galileo and Hobbes, affects our perception of secondary qualities. It does not consist of our believing something to exist that does not exist—for secondary qualities such as colors exist. Rather, it consists of our mislocating the qualities; we project them upon bodies when they are really exemplified in the sensory appearances or sense data. So most of our beliefs about secondary qualities have an element of truth. When I think of some particular thing that is red, then, usually, something is red, though the item to which I attribute the color does not have it.

There is, however, another possible account of the great deception of sense, and that is the claim that nothing has any secondary qualities at all. Colors reside neither in the object nor in consciousness nor in anything else for that matter. Our perception of colors is hallucinatory. This is the view that, I shall argue later, is more plausible than any of the other historically more predominant accounts of secondary qualities. It denies that we need any theory of matter or mind that finds room for secondary qualities. This is its great advantage, particularly as far as the mind is concerned. For how can colors, for example, reside in consciousness? The most natural interpretation of the claim that red exists in some item is that that item is itself red. But how can a mental event exemplify a color? Whatever has color has shape. Can mental events or states have shape?

The problem cannot be dissolved by adopting a materialistic theory of the mind as did Hobbes. With dualism, the mind is conceived either as an unextended substance or as a series of nonextended states and events. It is inconceivable that such items can exemplify colors. On a materialistic theory, the mind is identified with the brain or with states of and events occurring in the brain. It is not inconceivable that there be a red spot in the brain whenever red appears. The difficulty is an empirical one: in perception, what goes on in the brain are electrical and chemical changes; the apparent secondary qualities themselves are not exemplified there. The brain state that is the organic foundation of the sensation of red is not itself red; one who observes that condition of the brain will not see red.

So colors do not reside in consciousness or in the mind or in the brain by way of exemplification. Perhaps there are other ways they can be 'in' consciousness. In the course of his defense of his immaterialist view that both primary and secondary qualities exist only in the mind that perceives them, Berkeley suggests the following:

It may perhaps be objected that if extension and figure exist only in the mind, it follows that the mind is extended and figured, since extension is a mode or attribute which (to speak with the Schools) is predicated of the subject in which it exists. I answer, those qualities are in the mind only as they are perceived by it—that is, not by way of *mode* or *attribute*, but only by way of *idea;* and it no more follows that the soul or mind is extended, because extension exists in it alone, than it does that it is red or blue, because those colors are on all hands acknowledged to exist in it, and nowhere else.[11]

There are two ways that something can be in the mind: as a predicate of the mind or as an idea in the mind. For Berkeley, figure and color are in the mind as ideas, not as predicates. To say that I have an idea of red does not imply that anything in my mind is literally red. The question is whether we can develop an understanding of how colors can be in the mind as ideas. Whatever ideas are, they are not things that literally have colors or are colors. The idea of red neither exemplifies red nor is identical with red. Later we shall explore various accounts of how secondary qualities can reside in consciousness. Whatever ideas turn out to be, they must be the sort of item that can convey information (or misinformation) to the mind and thus serve as a source of knowledge (and error) about the external world.

The problem I shall discuss in the following pages is not that of Descartes's radical skepticism, but the more manageable one of how secondary qualities, and particularly colors, fit into our scheme of mind and matter. These reflections will lead us to consider several fundamental issues in the theory of mind and of human knowledge. The procedure I have adopted is to investigate various competing accounts of the nature of secondary qualities. We shall find that none of the standard accounts is completely satisfactory and that the search for a better approach will generate another kind of skepticism, namely doubts about the very reality of colors and other secondary qualities.

A good place to start is with Locke's theory, which has become the standard or dominant model. I shall call it *the pure power analysis.*

TWO

Locke's

Pure Power Analysis

At one point, Locke raises the question of the extent of our knowledge of "*the Powers* of Substances to change the sensible Qualities of other Bodies." Through sense experience we observe a great degree of regularity in the interactions of material bodies. He wonders whether we will ever discover to any great extent the unobserved and unobservable basis for perceived connections of qualities and changes. He agrees with "the corpuscularian Hypothesis, as that which is thought to go farthest in an intelligible Explication of the Qualities of Bodies; and I fear the Weakness of humane Understanding is scarce able to substitute another, which will afford us a fuller and clearer discovery of the necessary Connexion, and *Coexistence,* of the Powers, which are to be observed united in several sorts of them."[1]

Our notion of power is derived from our observation of constancies in the changes among bodies. We discover, for example, that fire has the power to melt gold—this is an active or causal power of the fire and a passive power of the gold.[2] Locke thinks that the corpuscularian hypothesis is the best current explanation of such regularities. If it were not for the active powers of bodies, we would never know anything about them, for our knowledge of matter is the outcome of its effects upon our bodies and minds. Coming to know is a special case of the actualization of active and passive powers.

Locke contrasts powers with real qualities. The primary qualities are real "because they really exist in those Bodies."[3] But other qualities are not real, because they are nothing but powers. The secondary qualities "are nothing in the Objects themselves, but Powers to produce various sensations in us by their *Primary Qualities*."[4] For example, when one judges of some object that it is red, one is asserting that it has the power to produce sensations or ideas of red in the minds of those who observe it. Why it has that power rather than some other is to be explained by the primary qualities of the corpuscles of which it is composed.

Primary qualities are powers as well. I am able to see that an object is, for example, square because it has the power to produce sensations of squareness in my mind when I look at it. But it is not true to say that its being square is nothing but this power. Its having this power is a consequence of its being square 'in itself'. Its being red, on the other hand is nothing but a power. Its having that power is a consequence of its primary qualities. Its being red is not something it has 'in itself'. We explain why something that is square looks square by reference to its being square. But we do not explain, according to Locke's theory, why something that is red looks red by reference to the fact that it is red. Rather, our explanations need to make reference only to its primary qualities. I

14

shall mark this distinction by saying that for Locke, the secondary qualities are *pure causal powers* whereas the primary qualities are *real*. A real quality has a nature of its own in virtue of which it has certain effects. A pure causal power, on the other hand, consists of nothing else but the fact that the subject in which it resides is capable of certain effects in virtue of its real qualities.

In general, a secondary quality is a causal power of a body to produce certain sensations in virtue of its primary qualities. This account of Locke's could not have been intended by him to be an analysis of our common sense understanding of the nature of secondary qualities. It is not a product of conceptual analysis. In the first place, it is derived from an application of the corpuscularian hypothesis to the physiology and psychology of sense perception and thus transcends the data available to common sense uninstructed by science. Second, Locke thinks that common sense has a mistaken view of secondary qualities. Our senses are liable to be deceptive because:

> the *Ideas of primary Qualities* of Bodies, *are Resemblances* of them; and their Patterns do really exist in the Bodies themselves; but the *Ideas, produced* in us *by these Secondary Qualities, have no resemblance* of them at all. There is nothing like our *Ideas*, existing in the Bodies themselves.[5]

Locke is saying here that our visual experiences represent bodies accurately with respect to the primary qualities but not with respect to the secondary. Bodies usually have the shapes they appear to have, but there is always some deficiency in appearance with respect to color.

Locke characterizes the deficiency as a failure of resemblance.

15

Colors as ideas, as aspects of inner appearances, do not resemble colors as qualities of bodies. The failure is radical; there is no resemblance at all. On a literal interpretation of "resemblance" according to which colors are taken to be exemplified by ideas and then compared to colors as exemplified by bodies, Locke's view is inconsistent with his claim that the mind and its contents are unextended. But there is no inconsistency if we take "resemble" to mean "represent"; such an interpretation is consistent both with Locke's language and his overall point of view.

Our ideas of secondary qualities, then, fail to represent them accurately. Our senses are systematically deceptive with regard to colors, sounds, and so forth. The respect in which secondary qualities are misrepresented concerns their classification under the category of power. Although they are "nothing but powers," nevertheless "they are generally otherwise thought of." They "*are looked upon as real Qualities, in the things* thus affecting us."[6] Common sense takes colors to be real or occurrent qualities, not to be causal powers or dispositions. We take colors to be something they are not. Our sensory apparatus represents colors to us as if they were real. Perception causes us to miscategorize them. The red that appears in my visual experience is taken to be the very same red that I ascribe to bodies. But that is a mistake, because seen red is or is represented to be real, whereas, objectively, it is nothing but a power. Locke has nothing to say about how or why the misrepresentation occurs.

Locke's view is not exactly Hobbes's and Galileo's view of "the great deception of sense." Whereas Locke thought that secondary quality terms can be truly predicated of bodies, they asserted, on the contrary, that secondary qualities exist only in the mind and are erroneously believed to inhere in bodies. But perhaps the disagreement is more verbal than substantive. All three would agree that bodies possess the very causal powers that Locke calls the secondary qualities. All agree that colors do not exist in bodies just as they appear. So the difference seems to boil down to whether or not secondary quality terms should be used as names of the causal powers as well as of certain features of our sensory representation. I shall return to this question shortly.

Why did Locke think that there is this important difference between primary and secondary qualities? Why are shapes real and colors nothing but powers? The argument that he offers will be of fundamental importance in all of our subsequent discussion.

> And yet he, that will consider, that *the same Fire,* that at one distance *produces* in us the Sensation of *Warmth,* does at a nearer approach, produce in us the far different Sensation of *Pain,* ought to bethink himself, what Reason he has to say, That his *Idea of Warmth,* which was produced in him by the Fire, is actually *in the Fire;* and his *Idea of Pain,* which the same Fire produced in him the same way is *not* in the *Fire.* Why is Whiteness and Coldness in Snow, and Pain not, when it produces the one and the other *Idea* in us; and can do neither, but by the Bulk, Figure, Number, and Motion of its solid Parts?[7]

We would all agree that the pain that we feel upon approaching too close to the fire is in us, not in the fire. The example of the pain shows that we do not impute to bodies every quality that regularly and lawfully occurs in our experience of them. If someone were to claim that the pain is an objective quality of the fire that is merely apprehended by us, we could argue against him by referring to the fact that we can explain quite well why we feel the pain without supposing its objectivity. The explanation of the causes of pain brings in various features of the fire as well as of our bodies and nervous system, but at no point is pain to be included as one of the causes of the feeling of pain. The pain is thus shown to belong to the mental terminus of a certain transaction among bodies and not to the bodies that caused it.

Locke claims that the same argument that applies to pain also applies to heat, color, and the other secondary qualities. The explanation of our sense perceptions incorporates the corpuscularian hypothesis, according to which the only features of bodies that play an active causal role are the primary qualities. Physics has no need to impute any secondary qualities to bodies or to their minute parts. Apparent color is causally inert as far as physics is concerned. The only argument that can justify a claim that some quality or characteristic that appears has objective status is that the imputation of such status is an indispensable component of the best theories we have available to explain whatever occurs in nature and human experience.

The best theories that are available today would not completely agree with Locke's list of primary qualities. We can generalize Locke's concept of a primary quality as being the concept of those features of matter that are introduced by the best theories available at a given time. What is or is not a primary quality is thus relative to the development of science; our list of primary qualities can be expected to change with modifications in physics. We can add that an *objective feature of matter* is any feature introduced by those theories of physics that are true. We can at best conjecture what features are, in fact, objective. Normally we will think that the primary qualities on our current list are objective, but we may

18

well be mistaken in that supposition. In any case, it is plausible to assert that color does not occur on the current list of primary qualities any more than on the list derived from Locke's corpuscularian hypothesis. Thus we now have as good a reason as Locke had to insist that colors lack objective status.

In order for Locke's argument about secondary qualities to be able to support his conclusion about their lack of objective status, two additional assumptions must be added. The first is that the fact that a feature is introduced by our physics is sufficient for our having a good reason to think it has objective status. The second is that the same fact is necessary for us to have a good reason to think that it has objective status. Locke needs the second as well as the first in order to be able to rebut certain common sense arguments against his view. For example, suppose a philosopher was to argue that colors are as objective as shapes on the ground that we *see* colors in bodies just as much as we see shapes. As far as our ordinary sense perceptions are concerned, secondary qualities are on a par with the primary. This line of argument against Locke goes back as far as Berkeley. Locke can reply that our scientifically uninstructed perceptual judgments about what does or does not have objective status should be rejected if they fail to be supported by our physical theories. Sense perception is not an incorrigible foundation of human knowledge. In fact, our perceptual judgments themselves depend upon theories that, because they belong to the common sense framework of our thought, have been adopted without criticism and are not to be trusted. We shall examine such common sense arguments at greater length in Chapter Eight.

Why, we may well ask, do the theories of physical science play such a crucial role in the epistemology we have found in Locke? I suggest that, for Locke, epistemology must itself be grounded in science. Our knowledge of the external world is a product of the interaction of matter and mind. The details of this interaction are important for understanding the extent to which the data that get into the mind accurately represent the objective world. If we restrict ourselves to the data as we receive them, as Berkeley suggested, we have no basis for evaluating their accuracy. Because our psychology tells us that our sense data are produced by a variety of different processes—the transmission of various physical energies to the human body, chemical and electrical processes in the sense organs and nervous system,[8] and mental activity[9]—we have no way of telling, without a full understanding of these processes, which features of our data constitute reliable information and which constitute noise, distortion, and error. In his epistemology, Locke incorporates psychology into his account of what it is reasonable to believe, because only those beliefs are reasonable whose informational basis has been evaluated.

Locke's reputation both as a radical empiricist and as a philosopher of common sense is undeserved and unwarranted. He was willing to criticize and modify our common sense framework if it clashed with or failed to take into account the best scientific theories of his time. Nor did he argue that our sense data form the only basis of our knowledge of nature. In his advocacy and use of the corpuscularian hypothesis, he went well beyond what sense perception and common sense unaided by science are capable of delivering.

Locke's naturalized epistemology[10] appears to be open to certain fundamental objections. First, if one of the tasks of epistemology is to provide a basis for accepting or rejecting theories about the constitution of matter, can one justifiably make use of any of the theories of matter whose credentials are at issue? Second, if sense perception plays an indispensable role in providing evidence that serves to support or corroborate our scientific theories, doesn't the use of the theories to criticize sense perception undermine their very basis of support? These are large issues that I shall return to later in Chapter Eight when our discussion is further advanced.

THREE

Criticisms of the Pure Power Analysis

Let me begin by summarizing the ontology presupposed in Locke's account of an individual perceiver's veridical sense awareness of a red body. First, of course, there exists the body sensed as well as the corpuscles that compose it. Second, there are the primary qualities of the individual corpuscles and of the body taken as a whole. Third, there is the sense experience in the mind of the perceiver, what Locke variously calls a sensation or an idea. Fourth, there is the quality red insofar as it occurs in the sensation or idea. I shall call it *apparent red* or *perceived red*. Fifth, there is the power or disposition that the body has in virtue of its primary qualities to cause sensations of red in perceivers. This is red as a secondary quality, or *dispositional red*. The system of primary qualities in the red object that underlies the disposition I shall call its *microstates*. And, sixth, there is the actual causal transaction between the body and the perceiver in which the power is actualized. A full description of this causal transaction will make use of theories of physics, biology, and psychology.

Locke is not very clear about how apparent red 'occurs' in the sensation of red. What makes that sensation a sensation of *red*? How can we understand the fact that something's looking red and something's looking green are qualitatively distinct experiences? One might be inclined to say that the way a color 'occurs' in a sensation is that the sensation represents it. A sensation of red is a mental representation of apparent red. But I do not think that this is a correct interpretation of Locke's intent. For him, apparent red represents red as a secondary quality, and, as we have seen, represents it deceptively. The relation of representation holds from apparent red to red as a secondary quality, and not from the sensation to apparent red. There really is no good explanation to be found in Locke's work of how apparent red 'gets into' experience. He does not seem aware that there is any problem here at all.

It is necessary to qualify Locke's interpretation of red as a secondary quality in accordance with the spirit of his overall view. Red as a power in a body is a relational property. That a body is red is relative to the perceiver in whose mind is caused the sensation of red. Locke either ignored or was ignorant of the fact that different species of animal sense the world quite differently, that what characteristically looks red to humans may present quite a different appearance to other animals.[1] We take human experience as the basis of our human color ascriptions. That something is red is relative not simply to the experience of perceivers generally, but to the experience of normal human perceivers. That we take ourselves as the standard explains the fact that our everyday color ascriptions are unaffected by the differences in the sensory apparatus of different animal species.

Criticisms of the Pure Power Analysis

The difficulty that I wish to emphasize in Locke's view and in most other versions of the pure power or dispositional analysis is his classification of secondary qualities as dispositions rather than as real or occurrent qualities. Is red as ascribed to objects really dispositional? Locke admits that although it is (as he thought) dispositional, we believe it to be occurrent because we mistakenly identify apparent red—which is occurrent—with red as a secondary quality. We have a false belief about color as ascribed to bodies.

When we ascribe a color to a body, we must distinguish two beliefs that may both be involved in the thought underlying our ascription. If I say, "That is red," I believe first that that really does have the color red, and second that the red it has is an occurrent quality. Locke never thought of challenging beliefs of the first sort. He wanted to present a theory of perception according to which most of our secondary quality ascriptions are true. But given his argument that secondary qualities cannot be occurrent, he was required to interpret them as dispositional—and thus to reject as false beliefs of the second sort—in order to preserve the truth of beliefs of the first sort. We are now in a position to understand that there is another alternative: secondary qualities are occurrent but nothing has them. Or, more accurately, secondary qualities would be occurrent if they were exemplified, but nothing exemplifies them. This alternative, which is the one that I shall undertake to defend in what follows, was never a genuine possibility for Locke, because it conflicted with that residue of common sense that he wished to preserve.

I do not interpret this issue merely as a verbal one. It is not just a matter of whether we prefer to use the word "red" as the name of a dispositional quality of bodies. Some may prefer that use and some may not. Given that bodies do have the dispositions that Locke classifies as secondary qualities, we can call them by any names we like. The issue is not about the word "red" but about the color red. When, for example, in science we want to explain why bodies have or appear to have certain colors, there is some phenomenon—color—that is the subject of our inquiry. The issue is to understand what the inquiry is all about. Or when I see a certain shade of blue covering the surface of a jar, and I exclaim, "What a beautiful color!" I am referring to that shade of blue. What is the nature of that item at which I am pointing and which I impute to the jar? Suppose that that very item is an occurrent quality. Then for someone to say that the jar has a certain dispositional quality that he will call by the name "blue" is not to present an alternative theory of blue but to change the subject.

The issue then is: Are the colors of bodies dispositional? Are they pure powers as Locke thought? Imagine that you are looking at the light blue color of the jar. Is that shade of color that I now see and that apparently belongs to or is exemplified by the jar just a dispositional quality? This way of posing the issue is legitimate even if, as I shall argue, nothing has any colors at all. For the question concerns the category that some familiar quality would belong to were it exemplified. We know what the quality is through our experience of it. We realize that our experience may be deceptive and that the quality may fail to be exemplified as it appears. Nevertheless, even if the experience is deceptive, colors appear to us, and we can thus identify the type of item whose category we are puzzled about.

One piece of evidence against the dispositional view is that the names for colors as they occur in natural language are not dispositional terms. Compare the difference between "light blue" and "fragile." The latter means "can easily be broken." That it designates a dispositional quality can be known by reflecting on what it means, whereas "light blue" is no more dispositional in meaning than are "square" and "round." As far as we can discover by reflecting on meaning, colors are no more dispositional than are shapes. Of course, given what colors are, we can infer certain dispositions that are implicit in their nature. I know how most light blue objects would look in daylight. But this inference is not licensed by our knowledge of meaning but by our understanding of the nature of color; knowing what colors are, we know how they characteristically look.

This argument against the dispositional view is by no means conclusive. It is logically possible that something can be dispositional in essence even though this fact about it is not incorporated in the meaning of its name. It is conceivable that something's metaphysical category is not semantically fixed but is discovered by inquiry and argument. Some philosophers—Whitehead and Russell, for example—have argued in various places that our language can be metaphysically misleading;[2] others—Spinoza and Hume, for example—have endorsed metaphysical ideas that have the consequence that our semantics is not an accurate guide to categoreal structure. It is proper to appeal to ordinary language and to what we say and mean as evidence to support philosophical claims, provided we recognize that such appeals do not infallibly settle the issue.

Ordinary language also fails to support another implication of the dispositional theory. If our meanings did incorporate the content of the theory, then color terms would be ambiguous: they would mean one thing when ascribed to bodies and something else when ascribed to appearances in order to reflect the categoreal difference between dispositional and apparent color. But there is in fact no such duality of meaning to be discerned. Suppose something both looks blue and is blue. Then the color it appears to have is the very same color that it does have. Our language incorporates the thought that apparent and objective colors are the same, that the very same quality that appears may also be exemplified by a body just as it appears. Given his view that the senses are deceptive in just this respect, Locke could agree that language does not reflect the duality between apparent and objective color while holding that language is misleading. He would certainly have to reject the appeal to ordinary language if it is taken to be the final word on the subject.

Another argument against the dispositional theory of color can be based upon the ways colors are 'in' the items that exemplify them. The light blue color of the jar *covers* its entire outer surface. The orange color of a carrot *pervades* it through and through. The blue color of the sky *fills* every visible region. In such descriptions, we speak of colors as covering surfaces, pervading objects, and filling spaces; we are treating colors as occurrent rather then dispositional qualities. Something that is capable of filling, pervading, and covering things seems as real as the things filled, pervaded, and covered.

There is a further argument that, when added to these somewhat inconclusive considerations, spells the end of the dispositional account. It is of the essence of a disposition that it may possibly not be actualized even when it is capable of being actualized. Not everything that is fragile is broken; not everything that is soluble dissolves. But what then is a disposition or a pure power? How is a dispositional quality to be distinguished from nothing?

The dominant view is that the form of speech in which we best express those dispositions that are causal powers in objects

—powers to produce certain results under certain conditions or powers to be affected in certain ways under certain conditions— is the counter-factual conditional. Thus to say that sugar is water-soluble means that if it were placed in water, it would dissolve. Such counter-factuals introduce causal connections into our discourse. To assert this counter-factual of a particular lump of sugar is to impute to it a certain causal possibility: its being placed in water would cause it to dissolve. On one version of this account, what justifies such an imputation is our knowledge of a law of nature. Because it is a general law of nature that things having a certain molecular structure D (or some disjunction of structures) dissolve when placed in water, and because sugar has D (or some member of the disjunction), we are justified in believing that this sugar too will dissolve when placed in water.

One may object that, after all, one may be quite certain that this lump of sugar would dissolve in water without having any knowledge of its molecular structure. What makes us certain that it would dissolve is that lumps of sugar just like this one have invariably been observed to dissolve whenever placed in water. So there is no need to appeal to a law of nature in this instance. Observed regularities suffice to justify our belief.

However, the observed regularity may be accidental. It is allowable to extrapolate a regularity to unobserved instances only if it is reasonable to think that it is not accidental, that it is an instance of a law that represents a necessary connection. Unless I believed that there was something about this sugar (I may not know what it is) which is such that its being placed in water would necessitate its dissolving, I would have no justification for taking past dissolvings as indications of how this lump would behave.[3]

Suppose someone claims that the fact that all A are B is a law of nature. How can that claim be supported? There are deep dis-agreements among philosophers of science about the confirmation of universal generalizations and statements of natural law. At mini-mum we can say that the mere fact that observed As have been found to be B is not sufficient to justify saying that "All A are B" ex-presses a law, because observed regularities do not, of themselves, suffice to establish causal regularities, as Hume has argued. What we need to do at least is to try to falsify "All A are B" by so varying conditions as to produce an A that is not B. If attempts at falsifica-tion fail, then it is reasonable to conjecture that it does express a genuine law.

According to the dispositional theory as here elaborated, that the jar is blue consists in the fact that it is such that its being looked at by normal human observers under conditions that make it and its properties clearly visible would cause it to appear blue to those observers. So for me to know here and now that this jar is blue, it is not enough that it look blue to me, a normal observer with unimpaired vision, when it is there, in a good light, right before my eyes. I need to know, in addition, that there is a law of nature such that looking at it under such conditions causally necessitates its appearing blue. And to know that, I must be apprised of all the circumstances necessary for the support of a claim that there does indeed exist such a law of nature.

It is, I think, clear that the dispositional theory requires too much for me to know in knowing that the jar is blue. On the contrary, for me to be able to tell that it is blue, all I need to know beforehand is how to identify blue, how to tell it from other colors. And to know this, it is sufficient that I know what blue things characteristically look like. When someone has this type of knowledge, she has a conception of blue. If I have a conception of blue, all that remains for me to tell whether or not something is blue is to look at it; in seeing its blue color and in knowing what it is for something to be blue, I am in a position to acquire the knowledge that it is blue. It is not necessary that I know or be apprised of any laws of nature about the causal powers of blue things. Of course, in order for me to see something that is blue, my senses must be affected, the object's causal powers must be actualized, and a law of nature must be instantiated. But I need to know nothing of this in order to learn, by seeing, what color it has. The colors of things can be seen straight away by looking at them. And this fact about the nature of color is not compatible with the way the dispositional theory characterizes it.

FOUR

The Microstate Theory

There is a hint of a different theory in Locke. In one place, he argues that a stone such as porphyry that is normally visible has no color in the dark, because, in the dark, it is incapable of producing apparent color.

> It has, indeed, such a Configuration of Particles, both Night and Day, as are apt by the Rays of Light rebounding from some parts of that hard Stone, to produce in us the *Idea* of redness, and from others, the *Idea* of whiteness: But whiteness or redness are not in it at any time, but such a texture, that hath the power to produce such a sensation in us.[1]

In this passage, Locke identifies color in an object not with a pure power but with a "Configuration of Particles" or texture or microstate that explains why it has these powers. According to the microstate analysis, colors are occurrent states of bodies, not mere dispositions.

The major historical representative of the microstate analysis is Thomas Reid. He appreciates the fact that his view is a further development of Locke's. "Upon the whole, Mr. Locke, in making secondary qualities to be powers in bodies to excite certain sensations in us, has given a just and distinct analysis of what our senses discover concerning them."[2] This praise of Locke is not unqualified. Locke's account of secondary qualities tells us what we learn by means of our senses. But what we learn of them in this way is quite limited because our senses fail to discern their nature. "Their nature not being manifest to the sense may be a subject of dispute. Our feeling informs us that the fire is hot, but it does not inform us what the heat of fire is."[3] Science, whose theories are not limited to "what our senses discover," has made some progress in revealing the true nature of secondary qualities. For example, "it has been discovered, that the sensation of smell is occasioned by the effluvia of bodies; that of sound by their vibrations. The disposition of bodies to reflect a particular kind of light, occasions the sensation of color."[4] Reid cannot accept Locke's pure power analysis, for it is not compatible with the thought that secondary qualities have an actual nature of their own that may be discovered by scientific inquiry.

Like Locke, Reid does not think that our senses are generally deceptive with respect to the primary qualities. "Our senses give us a direct and distinct notion of the primary qualities, and inform us what they are in themselves." But our senses leave the secondary qualities in obscurity. "But of the secondary qualities, our senses give us only a relative and obscure notion. They inform us only, that they are qualities that affect us in a certain manner—that is, produce in us a certain sensation; but as to what they are in themselves, our senses leave us in the dark."[5] Whereas we are directly acquainted with the primary qualities and thus are in a position to form a clear idea of them on the basis of sense experience, the only information about the secondary qualities that we are able to glean from the senses is that there is something not directly observable in the object being perceived that causes the sensation we receive when we perceive it. The red color of a body is not to be identified with apparent red. The latter belongs to the sensation and is something with which we are directly acquainted. The former is an unknown, but not unknowable, microstate of the body. It can become known only through a process of reasoning whereby theories are arrived at that adequately explain the causes of our sensations.

According to Reid, when we perceive an object, we must distinguish the perception from the accompanying sensation. He analyzes the concept of perception by reference to three necessary conditions: first, in perception, one has a conception of the item perceived; second, one believes that it exists; and third, this belief is not the effect of reasoning.[6] Sensations, on the other hand, do not contain any conceptions and beliefs; they are mental occurrences that accompany our perceptions.[7] In fact, "every different perception is conjoined with a sensation that is proper to it. The one is the sign, the other the thing signified."[8] In ways that we do not yet understand, events in the brain produce sensations that themselves cause perceptions.[9]

Reid is not, I think, correct in his view that sense perception essentially includes concepts and beliefs. A person can see something of which he knows nothing and of which he has no conception at all. He may lack the background knowledge necessary for him to identify what he sees, or his seeing of it might have been careless and inattentive. One may not even believe that what one sees exists, when, for example, one sees something that one falsely thinks is a hallucination. Reid is confusing the beliefs and judgments that are directly founded upon our perceptions with the perceptions themselves. This point will be considered at greater length in Chapter Six.

Reid is following his predecessors in his view of sensation. Sensations are subjective mental events that represent or signify objects in a way that enables us to perceive and to acquire knowledge of them. Without sensation, objects can be thought but they cannot be given. Among the items that he classifies as sensations are bodily feelings such as pains.[10] We are, therefore, able to have sensations even in the absence of perception. Perception entails sensation, but sensation does not entail perception.

It so happens that certain types of bodily sensations are inextricably woven into certain of our sense perceptions. We are able to perceive things by touch, taste, and smell only as a result of our receiving sensations in the organs of these senses. A person can become aware of the smell of a rose, for instance, only upon receiving certain sensations in the nose caused by chemicals exuded by the rose. If one loses the ability to acquire these sensations, one thereby loses the ability to smell.

Bodily sensations are the predominant items in that class of experiences that I shall label *sensory consciousness*. We can understand how, in certain cases, sensory consciousness is necessary for *perceptual consciousness*. In these cases, perceptual consciousness includes, but is not exhausted by, sensory consciousness. I can only smell the smell of a rose if I receive a certain sensation from it. But my having that sensation is not sufficient for the perception of the smell of the rose. I can have that sensation even in the absence of the rose.

Reid's account of secondary qualities is probably correct when our perception of them is founded upon a bodily sensation. When a person smells the rose, he becomes aware of something in the rose to which his attention is carried by the sensation. Since the sensation of smell contains the information in virtue of which one becomes perceptually conscious of the rose and its odor, it is reasonable to say that the sensation is a sign of and represents that quality in the rose which is its smell. Someone unacquainted with the chemical causes of smelling would have no idea of what it is in the rose that he smells. He can give it a name—"the smell of this rose"—and he is directly acquainted with its effects upon his sense organ, but he has no conception of its physical makeup. All that he knows of it is that it is something that has this sensory effect. He has, in Reid's terms, only a relative and obscure notion of it. In the same way, Reid's theory appears to be correct when applied to heat and to tastes. Our senses do not reveal the essential nature of these secondary qualities.

Sight and hearing, on the other hand, are not founded on bodily sensations occurring in the eyes and ears. In seeing, one normally has no feelings in the eyes; in hearing, there are usually no sensations in the ears. Sensations can occur when the visual and auditory stimuli are very intense, as, for example, when one looks at the sun. But unlike touch, taste, and smell, bodily sensations are not necessary for the occurrence of the perception. If sensory consciousness consisted just of bodily sensations and feelings, we would have to conclude that the visual and auditory forms of perceptual consciousness do not incorporate sensory consciousness. But then, in these cases, how can objects be given?

A central feature of sensory consciousness is that it is susceptible of variations even when the quality perceived remains the same. The heat of a hot body may remain constant even though our feelings of heat undergo change as we move closer to or farther from it. Having a bodily location, therefore, may not be the essential feature of a sensory event. More broadly conceived, sensory consciousness consists of those conscious events that can vary even though the perceived item remains constant and that may even occur in the absence of perception. So understood, sensory consciousness is a necessary condition in sight and hearing as well. In order for someone to see something, the object must look or appear in some way; in hearing, something sounds in a certain way. How something looks or sounds is susceptible of variation, though the object remains constant. In general, sensory consciousness, insofar as it functions as a necessary condition of perceptual consciousness, consists of the ways in which objects and their qualities appear to subjects. Objects are given insofar as they appear. Perceptual experiences consist of these appearances.

Even though we can vindicate Reid's view that sensation is necessary for perception, nevertheless there are difficulties with his microstate theory of secondary qualities as applied to seeing and hearing. In the perception of heat, we know of heat only as the unknown cause of our bodily feelings. But in vision, our experiences present us with the colored object itself and with its color. From a phenomenological standpoint, visual experience presents us with the colored object itself and with its color. Visual experience provides us with a direct acquaintance with color. It gives us a "direct and distinct notion" of color in general and of the various hues, shades, and tints in particular.[11] A visual experience is not a bodily sensation. It is, in veridical perception, an awareness of a colored body. Color is presented along with the object that exemplifies it. In visual perception, color is not thought of as the unknown cause of an experience, but is given in it. It is color itself that appears. It appears not by itself but as interwoven with the primary qualities of shape and size. Color is as directly given as shape.

Thus, even if the microstate theory is correct when applied to certain secondary qualities, it does not seem correct as an account of color. Our senses inform us of color but not of the microstates of the bodies that explain why we see the colors we do see. Colors are the very paradigms of items that are capable of being seen. They are preeminently visible. But the microstates of bodies are not things that can be seen. They are too small to see except with the help of instruments. They are the wrong sort of item to be identified with color.[12] Anything that can plausibly be said to be color must be visible. It must be capable of appearing in a visual experience. We must be capable of seeing it. Microstates, however, are theoretical entities with which no direct acquaintance is possible. They cannot be seen.

One way of formulating this argument against the microstate theory is that color has a property—capable of being seen—that is incompatible with a property possessed by microstates—incapable of being seen. Items with incompatible properties must be distinct in virtue of the very nature of an incompatible property.

There is, however, a standard response to this type of argument. It goes like this: "When the properties ascribed to an object are founded upon mental or intentional states, this argument is invalid. Terms referring to the same thing may fail to be substitutable for one another *salva veritate* in statements that allude to mental states. Thus the very fact that some item x can be seen when it is described in one way (e.g., as a color) and an item y cannot be seen when described in different terms (e.g., as a microstate) does not entail that x and y are not identical. Perceptual statements constitute opaque contexts in which one cannot expect substitution *salva veritate* to be valid."

Later (in Chapter Six) I shall argue that when "see" is used as a verb for visual perception, the sentences in which it occurs are not opaque. But, however one decides this issue, it seems to me that when you really do have incompatible properties exemplified by x and y, then x and y cannot be the same. If "capable of being seen" and "incapable of being seen" express incompatible properties, they cannot truthfully be predicated of the same entity. When it is claimed that they can be predicated of the same entity, it is tacitly supposed that they do not really express incompatible properties; they only seem to. Something may be capable of being seen in one respect but not in another. So there is no actual incompatibility here. In the next chapter, I shall consider whether relativization to different respects can save the microstate theory.

Both Locke's pure power analysis and Reid's microstate theory fail for similar reasons. For both, merely looking at something in order to see its color is insufficient for determining what color it has. For Locke we must make use of those inductive procedures that are capable of corroborating the existence of a natural law. On Reid's view, we must invoke theoretical inferences from our sensations to their unknown cause. But, in fact, our knowledge of color is largely non-inferential. We *see* the colors of bodies and make judgments about them accordingly. A book's being red, for example, is a state of affairs that can be presented in visual experience. We learn that it is red in virtue of being acquainted with this directly given fact. Thus, our conception of perception fails to square with the account of the nature of color provided by either theory.[13]

There is a certain account of the meaning of color terms in our language that fits in nicely with these criticisms of the microstate theory. I shall call it the *standard account*. Color terms typically occur in sentences either as nouns or as adjectives. As nouns occurring in singular term positions, as in "Red is the color of my true love's hair," they function as names that are used to refer to colors. As adjectives, as in "The rose is red," or "That is a red rose," the situation is slightly more complex because adjectives are not, strictly speaking, names. Yet as either nouns or adjectives, color terms represent colors and are used to communicate and identify which colors are under discussion. In order to avoid confusing the name-relation with other modes of representation, I shall say that adjectival color terms signify rather than name colors. Both naming and signification are species of representation. The items that color terms represent are directly presented in experience; they can be seen. They are qualities whose very nature it is to be visible, to appear in a visual manner. One typically teaches the meanings of color terms by presenting the learner with colored items while uttering the appropriate term. The learner acquires the ability to distinguish colors from the other perceptible qualities that objects exemplify while at the same time associating the term with the appropriate color.

Color terms are not the only words that represent colors. For example, in "This exactly resembles the color of my kitchen wall," the phrase "the color of my kitchen wall" is used to refer to a particular color. It does so by imputing to the color a characteristic —namely the property of being exemplified by my kitchen wall— that it possesses only contingently. That color might not have been exemplified by my kitchen wall. If, instead, I refer to it by its name —say "light gray"—I am not imputing to it any feature that it only contingently possesses. In fact, I am not ascribing to it a feature it possesses; rather, I am saying what color it *is*. One who knows the English language and thus knows the meanings of the main color terms in English thereby knows which colors are represented by which terms. Knowing these facts about the terms is all there is to knowing their meaning. And knowing what a particular color is depends, for human beings in this world, on the color's having appeared in a visual experience.[14]

There is a certain argument due to Saul Kripke in support of the microstate theory that, at the same time, challenges the standard account.[15] It seems a fact that how objects appear with respect to their colors depends not only on what colors they have and not only upon the conditions of illumination but also upon the visual apparatus of sentient organisms.[16] Things that are yellow, for example, usually look yellow to us under conditions that now exist. Let us suppose that there occurs a slight change in the human visual apparatus or brain that has the consequence that yellow things come typically to look the way red things now look. When looking at something yellow, we 'see' apparent red rather than apparent yellow. We have, on this supposition, a sensation of red rather than one of yellow. That an object has a certain color is a state of affairs that is only contingently related to the color it appears to have. It is not a necessary truth or even an analytic truth that yellow objects look yellow.

Certain consequences are thought to be implied by this argument. First, the meaning of "yellow" is not determined by "looks yellow," because of the possible deviation of apparent from real color. Second, since the color we normally think an object has is influenced by the color it typically looks to have, then "looks yellow" fixes the reference of "yellow"; we take yellow to be that objective feature of bodies that, as a matter of fact, causes a sensation of yellow in human organisms. Third, colors are exactly as Reid thought them to be; they are microstates of bodies whose nature is not given to our senses but must be discovered by scientific inquiry. And fourth, it is not true, as the standard account asserts, that one who knows the English language and who knows, thereby, how to use "yellow" knows what yellow is. In fact, if the meaning of "yellow" is determined by the nature of yellow, then one who, in knowing English, knows the proper use of "yellow" may not know its meaning. Its meaning is known only to specialists who investigate the microstates of bodies.[17]

The cogency of this defense of the microstate theory depends upon a certain view of the nature of visual sensory consciousness. If a sensation of yellow were just a mental event, a subjective experience going on in the mind of the perceiver, an event quite separate and distinct from the items perceived by means of it, then there would be a gulf between objective and apparent yellow, a gulf that would support, at best, a contingent connection between them. On this view, it would be implausible to think that one who was acquainted only with the sensation would thereby know the nature of yellow as well as the meaning of "yellow." What yellow really is would be inferred, not given. The only role for the sensation of yellow would be to fix the reference of "yellow," not to determine its meaning.

This conception of visual sensory consciousness is not compatible with its phenomenology, with its structure as it manifests itself in our experience. Visual sensations possess a subject-object structure: they consist of an awareness of items that are directly presented.[18] One who has a sensation of yellow is presented with yellow, among other things. Moreover, the color that appears by means of the sensation is presented as a feature of a body or region of space; phenomenologically, visual consciousness reaches beyond the perceiver to the spatio-temporal world without. *Prima facie,* visual consciousness is a way of being in contact with the world. What is given is not, phenomenologically, a constituent of consciousness, but a feature of bodies accessible to anyone possessing the right visual apparatus. This, I think, is the more accurate account of our concept of visual consciousness.

The defender of the microstate theory may reply as follows: "You claim that colors are objective, that they are features or states of bodies. So far I agree with you. That is a correct account of the ways we speak and think about color. However, you claim that apparent color, the color that is directly presented in visual experience, is color. There I disagree for the reason that, as I have stressed, it is a function of our visual apparatus and nervous system and can vary while the real colors of bodies remain the same. Apparent color, then, is, in some way, a constituent of the visual experience, not a feature of bodies."

This is a powerful defense, but the facts about the causes of visual sensations on which it is based do not force us to adopt the microstate theory. These facts provide strong reasons for thinking that, contrary to what we usually believe, apparent color is not an objectively existing quality exemplified by bodies. These facts provide further support for the views of Locke and Hobbes that our senses are deceptive in regard to color. But it does not follow that real color is as the microstate theory claims. There is an alternative view that is both consistent with these facts and also sensitive to the arguments on the basis of which I have criticized the microstate theory. It is the view that there is no real color at all. Bodies appear to have color, but these appearances are deceptive. Colors as objective features of bodies just do not exist. The yellow that is presented to me when I look at a yellow pencil, that very apparent color which seems to me to cover the pencil's surface, is, to put it directly and simply, just a hallucination. Nothing exemplifies it. Since nothing has color, we do not have to look in the mind for it either; we do not have to worry how, if apparent color is not exemplified by bodies, it is exemplified by mental events or states. Neither our philosophy of nature nor our philosophy of mind has to worry about color exemplification.

The defender of the microstate theory may respond as follows. "You have shown that the facts about the causes of visual experience that I have relied upon do not provide conclusive arguments in favor of the microstate theory because there is an alternative view equally consistent with these facts, namely *skepticism about color*. But your alternative is incredible. How can anyone believe that color experiences generally are hallucinatory? On your view, every statement in which we ascribe a color to a body or region of space turns out to be false. Your view is a heroic measure that, fortunately, turns out to be unnecessary. We are as sure about the reality of color as we are about anything else. Even if you are correct that there is a difficulty in the microstate theory in its view about the nature of color, it is better to face the difficulty than to go to the extremes you endorse. Even if my view has the further difficulty of implying that apparent color must belong to consciousness in some way, there are various theories that can be used to explain, in a satisfactory manner, how the secondary qualities can 'reside' in consciousness. So the difficulties for the theory of mind that the microstate theory entails can be met."

The Microstate Theory

I shall not respond to this challenge here but shall take up the issues it presents later in the discussion. How can color skepticism be made plausible, given its radical challenge to common sense? What shall be said about the claim that colors can be said to be in the mind in some sense? Before we turn to such issues, we shall consider an interesting version of the microstate theory that promises to overcome some of the criticisms leveled so far.

FIVE

Theoretical Identification

The serious difficulties with the microstate theory that we have just surveyed lead to a very interesting revision of the theory that reveals the similarity of the problems we are discussing to very deep issues in the philosophy of mind.

One important difficulty was that colors, being visible, cannot be identified with microstates, which are invisible because they are too small to see. However, in science, it is not unusual to discover that an observable item can plausibly be identified with an item that is introduced by a theory whose terms refer to objects and events that are unobservable. Lightning is a standard example of this kind of theoretical identification. On the one hand, lightning is something that we can see. It is presented to us in our visual experiences. On the other hand, it is an electrical phenomenon whose properties are determined not by vision but by inferences based upon physical theory. A visible flash of lightning *is* an electrical discharge in the atmosphere. Its being an electrical discharge constitutes, in part, its nature or real essence.

Theoretical Identification

It would appear that in order to identify the visible lightning we see with an electrical discharge, we must recognize that the same event or physical phenomenon may have a plurality of aspects, some of which may become vehicles by which its existence and nature can become known. Because lightning has a visual aspect, it can be detected by visual means, just by looking at it. The only background information that one needs in order to tell just by looking that something is lightning is knowing what a flash of lightning looks like. But lightning has another aspect; it is an electrical event. This aspect cannot be detected just by looking but must be inferred from observable data on the basis of physical theory. In the case of lightning, we have a dual access to the same event; one access is visual and the other is based upon theoretical inference.

Some philosophers have relied upon the analogy with lightning and other cases of theoretical identification in science to make a case for the identification of the mind with the brain. A mental event (or state) *is* a brain event (or state), they say, to which we have a dual access; through introspection we have access to one aspect of the brain event; neuroscience provides a different access. The plausibility of this claim rests upon the supposition that what introspection reveals is an aspect of the very same event whose other aspects are discoverable through scientific inquiry.

The microstate theory can make use of the same argument made in the brain-mind case. The color red is both a visible quality that can be detected by looking and an invisible microstate of the bodies we see. As a visible quality, it can be detected without our relying upon any background knowledge other than what it looks like. As a microstate, it can be described and detected by scientific means. There is no contradiction in saying that colors are both visible and invisible provided we introduce the idea that colors have a plurality of aspects. They are visible in one respect and unobservable in another. The microstate theory of color is thus modified in order to take account of this plurality of aspects. A specific shade of red has a visible aspect (V), which we see when we look at the body that exemplifies it, and an unobservable aspect (M), which is inferable on the basis of theoretical considerations. Because color is an amalgam of both aspects (V plus M), in detecting either aspect we succeed in detecting the color itself.

Whereas the original version of the microstate account identified color with M alone, this new one asserts that color is M plus V; color is something that has these two aspects at least. I think, however, that this version is just as implausible as the first. Aspects as we have been speaking about them are items that can be separately identified and described. The microstate theory in this version is committed to their separate and distinct existence. It asserts a duality in the nature of color itself. Now, from one point of view, the visible aspect drops away as irrelevant, for it plays no role in color perception; it is M that does all the work. This returns us to the first version, according to which color is simply the microstate M. But from another point of view, the microstate drops away as irrelevant, for, given V, we have what is both necessary and sufficient for us to see color and, therefore, for something to be color. In addition, if the co-occurrence of particular Ms and particular Vs is not accidental, there must be a lawlike relation between them. But all the items in the causal mechanism that could possibly account for the lawful association of M and V belong to the side of M. There seems to be nothing in physics that explains how M produces V or V produces M. M contributes to producing the appearance of V, but that is another story altogether. There is no simple way to get from the appearance of V to its independent and distinct existence.

Theoretical Identification

Our concept of color, the concept that is embedded in our non-technical thought and talk about bodies, space, and images, is the concept of a visible quality that can be directly observed. Modern physical and psychological theories of light and color have, since the time of Descartes, provided some reasonably successful though partial and incomplete explanations of why bodies display the colors they do and how we are able, with our visual apparatus, to perceive them. An important element in these explanations is a theory about those microstates of bodies—their specific atomic structures—that cause their differential reactions to light. These scientific advances are quite compatible with our common sense identification of color with the visible quality V, although, as I shall argue, they also provide reasons for thinking that our common sense concept of color is the concept of a quality that we discover to be unexemplified.

It is true that physicists occasionally speak of the physical basis of color as if it were color itself. The items that they frequently call colors are not the colors presented in our perception of bodies but the underlying structures and events that explain our perception. This new use of color terms is a semantic shift in which terms that have been and still are used to represent one sort of item come to be used, in technical talk, to represent items that are distinct from though causally implicated with the former. The simplest way to characterize this shift is to point out that when color terms are used in physical science to talk about microstates, they are no longer being used as names of colors. As science yields insight into the causes of color (or, more exactly, of apparent color), it does not require us to modify our concept of color. To say that color is not V but V plus M is at best a verbal recommendation that does not further the cause of clarity.

But what about the analogy with lightning? The defender of the microstate account will argue as follows: "It is reasonable to claim that discoveries about the underlying electrical properties of lightning tell us more about its nature or its real essence. If, after gaining this new understanding, we observed an event that looked like a flash of lightning but lacked its electrical properties, we would justifiably be puzzled, and we might well conclude that the event was not really lightning. Is it not reasonable to say the same of color? If so, then insight into the microstates of bodies can tell us not merely about the causes of color but about its nature or real essence."

The cases, however, are different. If we observed the color of a body that lacked the 'right' microstates, we would not doubt that it was color that we saw. We would have an anomaly that would prompt us to search for an explanation. But it would be an anomaly about the causes of color or apparent color, not about the causes of something else that only bore a striking visual resemblance to color.

There is a specific reason why the analogy with lightning fails to bolster the case for the microstate theory. A flash of lightning is an event, and, as such, it is a concrete particular that is capable of exemplifying a variety of distinct qualities and properties. Thus, there is nothing odd in the supposition that it possesses unobservable features that constitute its real nature. That it is a concrete particular implies that it is, in principle, inexhaustible in the number of qualities it is capable of exemplifying. It *has* qualities, but it is not itself a quality. In contrast to lightning, a color *is* a quality of the objects that we see. Because it is its very nature to be a quality, there is no distinction between its nominal and its real essence.[1] For this reason, it is implausible to claim that colors themselves are constituted out of a variety of aspects; that would be to treat them as particulars.

Whether or not the lightning analogy is helpful in establishing the identity of the mind with the brain depends upon what is being identified with what. If we interpret the relevant mental entities to be events and thus particulars, then the lightning analogy is helpful to the materialist, for it bolsters his argument that mental events are brain events. However, it is helpful at a cost, since even if a mental event is a brain event, it is a brain event that displays a duality of aspects, one of which is, apparently, irreducibly mental. So even if an identity of events can be justified by argument, mind can, nevertheless, be distinguished from body as a distinct aspect of brain events. If, however, the relevant mental entities are interpreted as qualities, as, for example, one might plausibly classify pain, then the lightning analogy is not so helpful to the cause of materialism any more than it helps the microstate theory establish the identity of a color with a microstate.

This criticism of the revised microstate account has proceeded on the assumption that V and M are numerically distinct items. If they are distinct, it is reasonable to doubt that color is to be identified with M or with M plus V rather than with V alone. But proponents of this account may find reason to reconsider this assumption. They may argue that when we see a particular color, we are actually seeing the microstate M; there is no V distinct from M at all. The following analogy may be used in support of this claim. We know how to cause people to see an uninterrupted expanse of color on a sheet of paper by covering the paper with colored dots. If the dots are small enough and sufficiently close together, we do not see them as dots but as a solid expanse.[2] What we are really seeing are the dots, although we might not realize it. There are not two entities here, the bunch of dots and the uninterrupted expanse, but only the bunch of dots. Similarly, it may be claimed, when we look at the red color of an object, we are seeing the very microstate M itself, which explains the color; we are not, however, seeing it as the microstate it is but as a smooth expanse of color covering the object's surface. We do not have two distinct items here, M and V, but only one, M, that is presented as a visible color expanse.

This analogy may also be thought to support mind-brain identification. When I feel a pain, it may be argued, I am actually conscious of the neural event that is the pain; I am not, however, aware of it as a neural event in all its complexity. It presents itself to me in my consciousness as a pain. In general, conscious awareness presents items that are complex and heterogeneous as simple and homogeneous.

The analogy, however, is persuasive only because it is incorrectly characterized. In the case of the colored dots, we are affected with a sensory illusion. We think we see a smooth, uninterrupted expanse of color, but, in fact, there is no such thing; there is only the bunch of dots. So it is a mistake to claim that the expanse of color really is the same as the bunch of dots, for this implies, incorrectly, that there actually exists a smooth expanse of color. It only seems that way. Instead of supporting the implausible claim that colors are microstates, the case of the colored dots, when correctly described as the illusion it is, supports the view that colors do not really exist,[3] that our perceptions of color are hallucinations in which we are caused to think we see something that is not there at all.

Nor does the analogy bolster the case for mind-brain identity. For suppose that the pain really is a neural event. Nevertheless, it does not seem to the sufferer to be a neural event but to be a pain. So in addition to there being a neural event, there is another distinct event, namely its appearance as a pain. The result of 'reducing' the mind to the brain is the reappearance of the mind as the very consciousness of the brain itself. In the case of color, I suggested that the best way of interpreting the analogy justifies the conclusion that color perceptions are hallucinatory. But that maneuver is not available to the materialist in the mind-brain case. Color perceptions are hallucinatory because color perceptions are not veridical. But even if the awareness of pain contains an element of hallucination, there still exists the pain experience, which, it is alleged, fails to be veridical. Whereas color can be eliminated by reference to the non-veridicality of color experience, reference to the non-veridicality of pain experience presupposes the existence of conscious experiences and impedes the attempt to eliminate them.

SIX

Consciousness

There is another view of secondary qualities to be considered, the one that we found in Galileo when he said that "they reside only in consciousness." In what sense can colors be 'in' consciousness? I shall take up this question in the next chapter, and in this I shall undertake to examine the notion of consciousness itself.

Although the term "consciousness" has received a variety of uses in the literature of psychology and philosophy, I wish to avoid merely verbal disputes, so I shall stipulate at the outset that I will use the term primarily to include what I earlier labeled as sensory and perceptual consciousness. Sensory consciousness includes bodily sensations and feelings as well as visual and auditory appearances. In order to distinguish perceptual from sensory consciousness, I need to say a few words about perception generally.

A perceptual verb such as "see" or "hear" marks, as has often been noted, something like an achievement or a success. When one sees an apple, then there really is an apple that is seen, whereas it does not follow from the fact that it looks to me as if there is an apple before my eyes that there actually is one where I seem to see it. The achievement consists in just this point of difference between seeing and 'mere' appearance, namely that what is seen exists and what appears may or may not exist.[1]

Cases of someone's seeing something, therefore, are relational facts. There is the person or organism that is seeing, there is the thing seen, and there is a relation between them that consists in or is founded upon the former's seeing the latter. When I speak of visual consciousness as something that is distinct from seeing, I intend to mark those constituents of the relational fact that belong to the one who sees in abstraction from the thing seen. When one sees something, one is visually aware of it in the manner characteristic of seeing. Visual consciousness is just one's awareness of it in abstraction from that of which one is aware. One way to mark the difference between seeing and visual consciousness is to represent them by the distinct formulas:

(A) X sees Y.

(B) It looks to X just as if X were seeing Y.

To mark the fact that in speaking of visual consciousness, I am speaking of what belongs to the subject in abstraction from the object, I shall speak occasionally of the subject's visual experiences. The initial justification in introducing visual experiences as actual entities and as real events in the biographies of perceiving organisms consists in the fact that whenever a subject is led to believe that he sees Y, it is logically possible that there is no Y to be seen but that what leads him to think that he sees Y—it is just as if he were seeing Y—is something that is happening to him.

56

Even though (B) does not entail the existence of objects of which
X is conscious, nevertheless the visual experiences that its instances
report are characterized with the help of names of perceptible objects. Because Macbeth's "fatal vision" was only "a dagger of the
mind," to his question, "Is this a dagger which I see before me, the
handle toward my hand?" the proper answer is, "No! It just looks
to you as if you were seeing a dagger with its handle toward your
hand." The reason we describe his experience in this way is that
we have no other way of easily and economically characterizing
it except by pointing out its resemblance to the experience one
characteristically receives when one really sees a dagger.

Some philosophers are willing to say that Macbeth's experience
has an *intentional object,* though not a real one. There is no harm
in thus introducing the notion of an intentional object, provided
we understand that it does not refer to shadowy existents that are
replicas of items that can be seen, but is a short-hand device for
characterizing experiences, a device that can be replaced by the
deliberately non-committal formula (B).

Earlier I distinguished perceptual from sensory consciousness by
reference to the fact that through a sequence of perceptions, the
object can remain constant even though the appearances vary. The
same thing can appear in various guises. This distinction can be applied to visual experiences in the following manner. Phenomenally
distinct (i.e., distinct in respect to the way something appears)
experiences may have the same intentional object. To classify an
experience as an instance of visual *perceptual* consciousness is to
identify it with respect to its intentional object. To classify it as
an instance of visual *sensory* consciousness is just to allude to the
fact that its constituents can change even though the intentional

object remains the same. More simply, many different possible experiences can be described by "it looks to Macbeth as if he were seeing a dagger."

The statement:

(C) It looks to Macbeth just as if he were seeing a dagger

says something about Macbeth. It ascribes a conscious visual experience to him and characterizes it with reference to its intentional object. In some recent philosophical discussions, a conscious experience of an organism has been described, somewhat awkwardly, as an event in which there is something that it is like for that organism.[2] One reason for finding this description to be of philosophical interest is that it raises a difficulty in reducing the mental to the physical. "For unlimited expertise on the physical goings-on in the organism on the part of a biologist, neurophysiologist, or other scientist could go with a total incapacity to imagine what it was like to be that organism."[3] A purely physical understanding of the life and experiences of an organism necessarily leaves out of account "the phenomenal forms" in which its surroundings appear in sense perception.[4]

Those who favor the reduction of the mental to the physical usually assert that experiences are brain processes or that they are realized in or are states of the brain. Even Shakespeare in describing Macbeth's hallucination has him say of his "dagger of the mind" that it is "a false creation, proceeding from the heat-oppressed brain." That the issue of reduction can be posed in these terms results from a variety of considerations.

First, how something looks to a person is a fact about him that does not consist of facts about his observable behavior, including his verbal utterances. What was happening to Macbeth in his hallucination cannot be literally observed by someone who sees Macbeth but must be inferred from what he says and how he acts. Second, Macbeth and only Macbeth has direct access to the fact reported by (C). It is quite unnecessary for him to observe his own behavior or to make any inferences from premises verified by observation in order for him to know that (C) is true. It is sometimes said that a person can know of his own experiences by introspection, but if we are to adopt this way of speaking, it must be with the understanding that the term "introspection" is just the name of this fact of direct access and does not contribute to its explanation. I shall mark these two points about conscious experiences in the usual way by saying that experiences are *private*.

The brain gets into the picture as a result of an empirical hypothesis. It was formulated long ago by Descartes when he said: "Only the brain can act upon the mind."[5] Normally, perceptual experiences occur when external forces impinge upon our sense organs. However, according to the hypothesis, in order for experiences to occur, the affected sense organs must first produce events in the brain, and if such events were caused to occur, even in the absence of the external forces, the experiences would also occur.[6]

Given the brain's central role in producing experiences, there are two main reasons favoring the reductionist claim that experiences are brain events.[7] The first is that if they are numerically distinct from the brain events that cause them, or from the brain events that they cause, we cannot understand how events so different can interact with one another. We are able to understand a causal sequence when we know enough to follow the linked series of events step by step and to explain by reference to some mechanism or underlying process how the later events emerge from the earlier.

In this way I understand why my car moves when I press down on the accelerator. But there are no known links that connect the brain with the mind. It seems as if the brain itself is a mechanism sufficient to produce the variety of human behavior, so how can the mind get into the picture at all? Of course, one may claim with Hume that, *a priori,* anything can cause anything, that only experience can tell us what actually causes what, and experience tells us of causal links between brain and mind. It is, the anti-reductionist may claim, a brute empirical fact that brain events cause experiences. Such causation is immediate and does not presuppose any intervening links or underlying mechanisms or processes. So the failure of mind-brain interaction to be 'intelligible' does not tell against it. Some causal connections are just brute facts and must be accepted as such without explanation.

This reply to the reductionist *may* be true. But the difficulty with it is that it is premature and that it blocks the road to inquiry. For if we accepted the argument, we would no longer have reason to search for links between mind and brain, we would have no reason to suppose the mind to belong to the central nervous system, and so we would lose the opportunity to investigate further into how neural events could accomplish what we know experiences accomplish. Reductionism, on the other hand, by supposing that there are links within the central nervous system between brain events and experiences, is capable of motivating fruitful programs of research. As Spinoza has said in arguing that "mind and body are one and the same thing": "nobody as yet has determined the limits of the body's capabilities: that is, nobody as yet has learned from experience what the body can and cannot do, without being determined by mind, solely from the laws of its nature in so far as it is considered as corporeal."[8]

The second reason in favor of reductionism is that if experiences are not brain events, then they are quite mysterious and do not seem to fit into any plausible scheme of reality. Sentence (C), for example, is a typical description of an experience. What other features does the event described by (C) have in addition to those to which Macbeth has direct access? If an experience exemplifies phenomenal qualities as some think, what is it exactly that does the exemplifying? Does it occur in space? If it does, where does it occur? If it does not, how can it be the experience of a definite individual? The fact that anti-reductionism provides no plausible answers to these entirely reasonable questions suggests that it is more productive of mysteries than understanding. We cannot exclude the possibility that anti-reductionism may someday produce a defensible metaphysical scheme in which both physical and mental entities are shown to be distinct parts of a common universe. But we do not have such a scheme now.

Despite these convincing arguments in favor of reductionism, there is a convincing reason against it. If experiences are brain events, then the content of (C) or, at least, part of its content, must be descriptive of some of Macbeth's brain processes. But a brain process is just a physical-chemical event; it consists of electricity and molecules moving in and among nerve cells. How can such an event constitute the appearance to Macbeth of a dagger? How can it *be* that very appearance? How do appearances and sensory events enter into electricity and molecular motion? How can there be room, in the very same event, for both physical and phenomenal features? And if the very same event does indeed exemplify both types of feature, have we not preserved the duality of mind and body as a duality of features rather than events? In the very process of overcoming one form of dualism, have we not stumbled into another? Just as the arguments in favor of reductionism show that we do not understand how mind and body can be separate parts of the same universe, so these questions show that we do not understand how mind can be included within the physical universe. We cannot exclude the possibility that reductionism may someday produce a metaphysical scheme that renders such a fit intelligible, but we do not have one now. So it seems that we have a genuine philosophical antinomy on our hands.

One way of overcoming the antinomy is to reject the assumption common to both reductionist and anti-reductionist positions that consciousness exists.[9] Such a view—sometimes called *eliminative materialism*—claims that sentences of type (C) are one and all false. Since there are no such events as experiences, the question whether experiences are or are not brain processes does not arise. The fact that we believe in the existence of experiences and that our beliefs about particular experiences of our own are immediate or non-inferential does not conclusively establish that there are such things, since important sets of human beliefs have previously been shown to be false, the product of ignorance and superstition.

One reason in favor of eliminative materialism has just been discussed: that it provides an escape from an antinomy that otherwise appears intractable. The other reason in its favor is founded upon a scientific hypothesis (H) that says that everything that occurs in the life of a living organism—including behavior and speech acts, among which are introspective reports—can be explained completely in physical and chemical terms. From the standpoint of explanation, the mind drops out of the picture entirely. And that means that there is no need for, no argument in favor of, the existence of experiences. Just as we no longer need to suppose that there are demons in order to explain epileptic fits, so, in the light of

(H), there is no need to suppose that there are experiences in order to explain sense perception. Thus, in order to argue for materialism, there is no need any longer to show that some brain events are experiences.

One trouble with this argument is that we do not know that (H) is true. Of course, advocates of (H) may argue that it is reasonable to suppose that we will sometime in the future be in a position to know (H), or at least to know that (H) is well-supported on the grounds that science is tending to provide explanations of more and more phenomena couched in purely physical terms. (H) reflects the general direction of science since the seventeenth century. What was once thought to be caused by spirit is now understood in terms of matter. So, it is argued, eliminative materialism is the most likely outcome of scientific inquiry.

The difficulty is not just that we do not now know that (H) is true. It is rather that we now have evidence that shows it to be false. The evidence consists in the fact that experiences play an apparently indispensable role in our explanations of human events. "What makes you think that his tie is pink?" "Well, it looks pink." "Why did you remove your coat?" "Well, it feels very warm in here." "What makes you think that there is something wrong with your eyes?" "I see black spots all the time." These are just a few of the countless instances in which we mention experiences to explain why we think and act as we do. If we were forbidden to offer such explanations, we would not know what to say. In addition, we now have no reason to think that our use of such mentalistic explanations clashes with any theories that the evidence obliges us to accept. Of course, if (H) were now part of our system of beliefs, there would be a clash. But the fact that mentalistic explanations pervade our forms of life and that there is now no known alternative to them is a good reason for excluding (H). We cannot be sure *a priori* that science will never tip the balance in favor of (H). But we are now entitled to reject (H) in the light of our best current explanatory practices.

Perhaps there is another way to escape from the antinomy. One difficulty with reductionism is that we do not know how to 'fit' experiences into the brain. How can a physical event such as a brain process also exemplify phenomenal qualities? How can a visual experience or a pain be realized in an electrico-chemical event? Now, there is a similar problem with respect to language. When I type the sentence (S) "The cat is on the mat," I am producing a physical object that consists of a string of marks made out of ink. Yet this string also possesses certain semantic features. The marks are grouped into words, each of which has a meaning. Certain phrases refer to various objects. The sentence as a whole represents an existing state of affairs, and thus is true. Meaning, reference, representation, and truth are semantic features that can be realized in material objects produced by human beings in the course of writing and speaking. A sentence, or, more precisely, a sentence token, is susceptible of two distinct dimensions of description. It can be characterized in terms of physical or semantic properties. Physically it is composed, say, out of black ink; semantically it represents the fact that the cat is on the mat. We have no reason to think that the semantic features are reducible to the physical ones. In fact, it is a puzzle how certain physical objects come to have semantic features at all. But there is no doubt that they do. Though meanings are different from shapes, there is no doubt that some things that have shape also have meaning.

These facts about language can be used to support the reductionist's claim that experience can 'fit' into brain events. For suppose experiences are realized by certain brain events just as semantic functions are realized by sentence tokens. Perhaps these brain events may be understood as analogues of sentence tokens with a structure analogous to the syntax of natural language and with elements similar to the words and phrases of natural language.

The philosophical tradition contains the thought that corresponding to speech formulated in one of the natural languages, there is mental discourse that speech expresses. Thus Aristotle writes: "Now, spoken words are symbols of affections in the soul, and written marks symbols of spoken sounds. And just as written marks are not the same for all men, neither are spoken sounds. But what these are in the first place signs of—affections of the soul —are the same for all; and what these affections are likenesses of —actual things—are also the same."[10] It appears as if Aristotle is saying that speech is able to represent actual things in virtue of its expressing in some way mental states—affections of the soul— that represent actual things directly. And Hobbes asserts that "the generall use of Speech, is to transferre our Mentall Discourse, into Verbal; or the Trayne of our Thoughts, into a Trayne of Words."[11] Similarly Locke says that "the Comfort, and Advantage of Society, not being to be had without Communication of Thoughts, it was necessary, that Man should find out some external sensible Signs, whereby those invisible *Ideas,* which his thoughts are made up of, might be made known to others."[12] We have, in these passages, the suggestion that the human mind contains mental representations and that speech acts acquire their representative capacity in virtue of some relation, not well specified in the writings of these philosophers, to their mental counterparts. There is also the suggestion that the system of mental representations constitutes a common language of thought[13] amidst the diversity of natural languages.

If there are mental representations, then it is reasonable to explore the hypothesis that the states of the brain are the tokens in which the mind's representational activities are realized. In fact, there is no other plausible hypothesis available. After all, the only stuff that the dualist has to offer is mind stuff, and all we know about that is that it is not the stuff of the brain or of anything else that physics is likely to stumble across. The mind stuff hypothesis seems to me to be a non-starter.

Moreover, there is good reason to think that there are mental representations. Take the case of belief, or, for that matter, of any propositional attitude. A person writes a sentence in order to make a statement, and, in making that statement, he expresses his belief. The sentence (S) can be used both to make the statement that the cat is on the mat and to express the belief that the cat is on the mat. A statement has a complex structure in which we can distinguish what it states—the proposition that is asserted to be true—and the activity of the speaker in making it. Within that activity, (S) is produced to function as the vehicle by means of which the proposition is expressed. Belief has an analogous structure. There is the proposition that is believed to be true, and it may very well be the very same proposition that is asserted to be true in the corresponding statement. In addition, there is a state of the believer, the fact that he believes just that proposition.

Normally we identify and individuate a particular belief state by specifying the proposition that is believed: "He believes that the cat is on the mat." We identify and individuate statements in the same way, as in: "He said that the cat is on the mat." Moreover, in describing what someone said, it is usually more important that we get the proposition right than its linguistic vehicle. But we frequently know what the vehicle is, for we are often in a position to observe it. However, introspection seldom reveals the nature of vehicles of belief. It is most likely that there are belief vehicles. To deny that would commit us to the implausible view that when a person believes two quite different propositions, there are no distinct facts of the matter about him that differentiate the belief states. Why are they two rather than one? How do they come to have different propositions as their objects? In order to answer these questions, we must appeal to some constituents of the belief states themselves, constituents that are analogous in structure and function to linguistic vehicles.

Even though the case in favor of there being mental representations and of their being identical with brain states can be rendered plausible, it is more difficult to substantiate the additional claim made by the classical account that there is a common language of thought. The language of thought hypothesis implies that the vehicles in the belief states that are analogues of the tokens of sentences in natural language are not tokens of the natural language of the believer but belong to a common human language of the mind, or *mentalese* as Wilfrid Sellars has called it.

One problem is that introspection occasionally reveals mental sentences that are tokens of sentences of natural language. When I think silently to myself, my mental discourse is in English. In fact, whenever I am introspectively aware of the vehicles of my propositional attitudes, I usually find that they are tokens of English sentences. And in those cases in which introspection fails to reveal the vehicle, cases in which I just do not know how I managed to express just that proposition, it is certainly possible that the vehicle was also in English.

There may be indirect evidence in favor of the common language of thought. If we had reason to suppose that animals or human infants are capable of being in belief states or instancing other propositional attitudes, then we would be entitled to conclude that there are mental sentences not in natural language, the exploration of which may justify the hypothesis of a common language of thought. This, however, is a topic that will take us far afield and will not be pursued any further in this place.

The central issue that concerns us here is whether or not perceptual consciousness in general and visual consciousness in particular can be plausibly interpreted as mental representations. The claim that they can be so interpreted I shall call the *representational theory of perception* (RTP). If RTP is true, then the argument for the reduction of the mind to the brain gains strength, and the central antinomy that constitutes the mind-body problem is on the way to being resolved.

One argument that may be thought to favor RTP is founded on the idea stressed in the phenomenological tradition that consciousness is always consciousness *of* something. It is always directed toward something. In judgment, something is judged; in desire, something is desired; in intention, something is intended. All these examples show that consciousness (now here broadened to include all mental states) essentially incorporates reference to or representation of objects. This is Franz Brentano's thesis that mental phenomena generally exhibit intentionality.[14] In the same way one may argue that perceptual consciousness exhibits intentionality. In seeing, something is seen. In hearing, something is heard, and so on. Doesn't this show that perception is intentional in its very structure? In perception, as in judgment, desire, and intention, a subject represents an object.

As it stands, this argument is not very persuasive. In order for it to justify RTP, it must establish that perception consists in the having of mental representations just as do judgment, desire, and intention. Yet the verbal similarities that the premise of the argument trades on—"In judging, something is judged, and in seeing, something is seen"—and that are summarized in the slogan "Consciousness is always consciousness *of* something" are not able to bear this weight. The verbal similarity may show that perception exhibits (as do the other cases) a type of subject-object structure. But it makes no headway at all in showing that the subject-object structure exhibited in perception is representational. Various structures may be comprehended under the concept of intentionality. On the face of it, perception is a type of presentational awareness in which objects are given or presented, whereas judgment and belief are not presentational at all.[15] The thesis of the intentionality of the mental summed up in the slogan "Consciousness is always consciousness of something" is far from entailing the representational character of consciousness generally.

Another quite different argument may be grounded upon the character of certain of our reports of experience. If I see something in a dim light, then, upon being asked about its color, I may respond by saying, "It seems to me to be blue." This report may be interpreted as an expression of my hesitant belief about its color, or even, less firmly, my inclination to believe. Cases of this sort provide a reason for claiming that perceptual experiences are just beliefs or belief inclinations and thus exhibit the same representational character as beliefs. Experiences are just those beliefs or belief inclinations that are produced in us by the impingement of energies upon our sense organs.[16]

The strength of this version of RTP lies in the fact that many of our experientially based reports do indeed express our tentative beliefs. If I am asked, "What color do you see that to have?" I may, after peering at the faraway and only dimly seen object answer, "It seems to me to be blue." And such a report can indeed express what I then and there think its color to be.

The difficulty with the argument is that the form of words in which the report gets formulated has nothing essentially to do with perception. I can use these words to express what I think when I am drawing a conclusion about the object on the basis of written data without having seen it. So the fact that I can use these words when I am looking at it and trying to discern its color fails to establish that what I am formulating is an experience. These words may, instead, constitute a conclusion I have drawn on the basis of my experience rather than a claim about its conscious content.

There are two reasons for thinking that experiences are not reducible in this way to beliefs. First, I can say that the object seems to me to be blue as an expression of what I take its color to be even though it does not look blue. It may look purple, but I know that, in this light, things that look this way are usually blue, so my tentative belief is that it is blue. Second, if, after saying that it seems to me to be blue, I am asked why I think it is, I can answer, "It looks blue." Since such an answer is not redundant and is indeed capable of explaining why I think it is blue, it is clear that such a report formulates my conclusion, not the experience that was its basis.

In addition, there is an epistemological reason for rejecting the claim that perceptual consciousness is a form of belief. A person's beliefs are frequently based upon other beliefs that constitute the evidence or reasons taken to support them. For example, my belief that this thing I am now looking at *is* blue may be based upon the fact that it *looks* blue. Also, I may *believe* that it looks blue and offer this as my reason for thinking that it is blue. But if asked for my reason for thinking that it looks blue, I may be unable to provide one except by saying, "Well, it just does." For I come to *think* it looks blue just because it looks blue. Its looking blue is not itself a belief or a thought but a directly presented state of affairs constituting a basis for confirming subsequent thoughts. If our beliefs did not terminate in such directly presented states of affairs that are not themselves beliefs, we would be unable to understand how any of our beliefs could legitimately claim to be true of the world that exists independently of what we believe it to be. For such claims to be legitimate, there must be non-accidental connections between the world and our beliefs. Perceptual consciousness is the basic medium in which such a connection is established.

So the identification of conscious experiences with beliefs that originate by means of the stimulation of the sense organs is not very promising. But perhaps there is a sufficient resemblance between experiences and beliefs to justify, in the absence of such an identification, the view that the former exhibit representational content as well. This is the line that John Searle pursues. He points out that not only are beliefs items that possess truth-value, but they themselves determine what counts in fixing their truth-value. The content of a belief determines what must be the case in order for it to be true and what must be the case in order for it to be false. "The Intentional content of the belief determines its conditions of satisfaction; it determines under what conditions the belief is true or false."[17]

Searle claims that visual experience resembles belief in just this respect. Like belief, visual experience can be correct (or veridical), or it can be mistaken (as in a hallucination).[18] For example, just because Macbeth knows that his experience is one in which it is just as if he were seeing a dagger, he knows what must be the case if his experience is to be veridical, and he also knows the conditions under which it is hallucinatory. The implication of this resemblance is that visual experience as well as belief exhibits representational content. Searle concludes that "the Intentional content of the visual experience determines its conditions of satisfaction; it determines what must be the case in order that experience not be a hallucination in exactly the same sense that the content of the belief determines its conditions of satisfaction."[19]

The argument, then, is this. The fact that beliefs have a truth-value is explained by supposing that they possess a representational content. Visual experiences can be either veridical or hallucinatory; these are features analogous to truth-values. So it is plausible to suppose that the same features that explain the truth-value capacity of beliefs are also exhibited by experiences.

By the same argument, Searle endeavors to establish that the content is propositional in nature. In order for a belief to possess a truth-value, it must express a proposition. "The content of the visual experience, like the content of the belief, is always equivalent to a whole proposition. . . . All seeing is seeing *that*: whenever it is true to say that *x* sees *y* it must be true that *x* sees that such and such is the case."[20]

There is a further point that needs to be added if this account is to be adequate. It is not enough to say that beliefs can be true or false in virtue of possessing a propositional content, because other propositional attitudes similarly have a content without being true or false. For example, in contrast to the attitude of considering whether or not a given proposition is true, belief affirms its truth.

That is why belief can either hit the mark with respect to truth or be mistaken. Since veridicality is taken by Searle to be analogous to or even to be the very same thing as truth, we must also suppose that visual experience affirms the proposition that constitutes its content. So visual experience not only exhibits content; it takes the content to be information about the perceived world.

Although Searle insists on this point of resemblance between belief and experience, he explicitly denies that the latter is merely a special case of the former. The reason is that "the experience has a kind of directness, immediacy and involuntariness which is not shared by a belief I might have about the object in its absence. . . . It is a presentation of that state of affairs."[21] But this argument against the belief theory of experience also raises doubts about Searle's own view. For if in seeing something, a state of affairs is presented, how can we say that it is represented? Searle insists that "presentations are a special subclass of representations,"[22] but that is odd, for the concept of representation would seem to be a concept that is determined by contrasting it to the concept of presentation. I can distinguish between an object or state of affairs insofar as it is given or perceived and the same object or state of affairs as a topic of judgment or belief. In the latter case it is represented, in the former presented. Classifying presentations as representations appears to be an *ad hoc* maneuver intended to save a theory that would otherwise be implausible.

There is another difficulty with the belief theory of experience that also tells against Searle's, namely that perception can occur without belief. There are two types of cases. One occurs when one sees something without knowing what it is that one is seeing. When I see a strange new object or a familiar object under difficult conditions, I may be unable to identify it and I may have no beliefs about it at all. It is presented in the visual field, but no thought about it gets affirmed. The second occurs when perception continues after we have ceased acquiring beliefs about what we see. Consider what happens when we look at a painting for the first time. At first, we are flooded with beliefs about the objects in the picture. But once we have satisfied ourselves about what it is we are seeing, we may continue to contemplate it just for the enjoyment. We look at things for pleasure as well as for instruction. These cases suggest that perception can occur even when no proposition is being affirmed or even considered; and this is incompatible both with the belief theory and with Searle's.

Searle's claim that visual experience has intentional content rests on his view that "all seeing is seeing that." One major difficulty here is that the "seeing that" locution has no semantic connection at all with seeing. Examples such as "Do you now see that 13 is a prime number?" show that "see that" expresses a cognitive concept similar in meaning to "realize that."[23] It would be more accurate to say: "No seeing that is seeing."

Another difficulty is that reports about what a person sees imply nothing about the propositional content of any of his alleged "seeings that." If, for example, Cicero sees Caesar, it does not follow that he sees that that person is Caesar or even that what he saw is a human being. "Seeing that" statements usually report cognitive achievements. When uttered in a perceptual context, they tell us what a person has learned on the basis of his perception. Reports about what is seen, however, simply tell us what is within an individual's field of vision. Whether anything has been learned as a result of this visual presence is another matter entirely.

First-person reports about what is seen do inform us about what is known. If Cicero should say in truth, "I saw Caesar," we would be justified in concluding not only that he saw Caesar but that he saw *that* the person he saw was Caesar. But the fact that such reports contain information about cognitive successes is a peculiarity of their being in the first person. It has nothing to do with the nature of visual perception as such. It is the fact that Cicero is able to tell us what he saw, not the fact that he saw it, that implies something of what he has learned.

In response to these criticisms, an advocate of RTP may retreat somewhat. He may concede that not all sense perception is representational, but he may insist that some of it is. He may claim, as does Fred Dretske, that in addition to non-epistemic perception as in:

(1)   Cicero saw Caesar,

there is an epistemic variety as in:

(2)   Cicero saw that Caesar is in the Senate,

which has propositional content and is a cognitive achievement.[24] However, this weaker claim is subject to the same difficulties as the former. For (2) says something like:

(3)   Cicero realized that Caesar is in the Senate.

So although (2) reports a cognitive state that has propositional content, it does not report a perception, though it may be based upon one. The concession that there are non-epistemic perceptions fails to make the case for epistemic perception any stronger. Once one agrees that there are non-epistemic perceptions, one can analyze the alleged occurrence of an epistemic perception as a true belief justified by a non-epistemic perception.

The view that there are perceptions that are representational is encouraged by the thought that facts or existing states of affairs are among the objects of sense perception. The types of visual object, of items that can be seen, are quite diverse. They include physical objects, their colors and shapes and other features, patterns, designs, relational structures, and unifying properties.[25] Also included are such items as shadows, reflections, and images. Among these frequently presented denizens of the visual world are facts. In his logical atomism period, Bertrand Russell often spoke of our acquaintance with facts. You can come to know, for example, that the sun is setting by inferring it from your knowledge of certain truths, but you can also come to know it by seeing the sun set.[26] You can acquire knowledge by acquaintance with the very fact whose existence you claim to know.

Suppose then that there is perceptual acquaintance with facts. One may come to think that such acquaintance must be representational. To take an example, suppose that one day, upon entering the Roman Senate, young Plautus witnessed Brutus stabbing Caesar. That Brutus stabbed Caesar is a fact. It seems reasonable to conclude that

(4)   Plautus saw that Brutus stabbed Caesar

reports his acquaintance with this fact. Because (4) implies that

Plautus learned and thus came to know that Brutus stabbed Caesar, it also reports a cognitive success, a case of knowing that. So it looks as if there are cases of perception that exhibit propositional content.

This argument, however, is mistaken. There are ways of recording Plautus' acquaintance with this fact or event that do not imply anything about what he has learned or come to know. For example,

(5)   Plautus saw Brutus' stabbing of Caesar

reports an event that occurred in Plautus' field of vision but does not tell us what he came to know as a result. For (5) could be true even if Plautus failed to realize that Brutus was doing the stabbing or that Caesar was the one who was stabbed. Moreover, (5) is consistent with Plautus' failing to recognize what it was that Brutus was doing to Caesar. Perhaps he thought that two men whose identities were unknown to him were locked in an embrace. (5) does not entail (4). Nor does (4) entail (5); perhaps Plautus entered the Senate too late to witness the assassination, but, seeing Caesar lying on the floor in a pool of blood and Brutus carefully wiping blood from his knife, he concluded that Brutus stabbed Caesar. So (4) can be true when (5) is false. (4) does not report Plautus' perceptual acquaintance with the fact it represents. Rather, it says that Plautus learned something—namely that Brutus stabbed Caesar —while remaining non-committal about how he learned it. (5) is quite definite about what Plautus saw but remains non-committal about what he came to know on its basis.

Up to this point, I have been criticizing those versions of RTP that say that perceptual experience exemplifies *propositional* content. There are other versions that stress the role of concepts rather than propositions. One of them stresses the selective nature of sense perception. What we say we see is a selection of items abstracted from the complex structures of the visual field. What we say we see is only a minute part of what we actually see. And what is directly presented in the visual field is itself a selection of aspects of items that are seen. The fact that what we see is seen under an aspect has been thought to provide a reason in favor of RTP. "All intentionality including the intentionality of perception is under an aspect," says Searle.[27]

In a paper on Husserl's theory of intentionality, Aron Gurwitsch develops this idea in detail. He distinguishes within all states of consciousness between the object that is intended or meant and the object *as* it is intended or meant.[28] He introduces, as does Husserl, the technical term *noema* to designate "the object meant and intended taken exactly as it is meant and intended."[29] In explaining this notion, Gurwitsch takes a particular linguistic paradigm as his point of departure. He relies upon the familiar contrast between meaning and reference as exhibited by definite descriptions. Two descriptions, different in meaning, may nevertheless refer to the same thing.[30] The referent is then intended or meant from a particular aspect or point of view. The difference in meaning is the basis of the difference of aspects.

Gurwitsch claims to find the noema in perception as well. The thing perceived "may be seen from different points of view—it may appear under a variety of aspects: from the front, the back, one of the lateral sides, and the like—while the perceptual noema denotes the thing perceived as presenting itself under *one* of those possible aspects."[31]

Suppose that Plautus used the description "the killer of Caesar" to refer to Brutus in the course of describing what he witnessed in the Senate. We can understand in this case what it means to say that Brutus is meant or intended under an aspect. In choosing this description, Plautus selected a concept to identify a particular person; he was led to select that concept by the information he wished to communicate. The person described is the locus of numerous concepts, but Plautus chose this one because of his communicative intention.

The question is whether something like this occurs essentially in sense perception. Suppose that when Plautus saw Brutus stab Caesar, he saw Brutus' back. Given Brutus' location and spatial orientation and Plautus' position relative to Brutus, he could only see Brutus from behind. The fact that Brutus' back was the part of Brutus that appeared in his visual field was no doing of his. No concept in Plautus' head is needed to explain why he saw Brutus from that point of view. The presence of a noema does not determine which part of Brutus was seen. Even if Plautus meant or intended to observe Brutus from his front rather than his back, he would, nevertheless, have seen his back, not his front, given their respective positions. Introducing a noema or conceptual element is unnecessary in order to explain the aspect (in the sense of spatial part) under which something is seen. Which part or aspect is seen is determined, given the position and orientation of object and perceiver, by the path of the light rays and the geometry of perception and has nothing to do with intentional content.

If a person sees something under an aspect, he may formulate what he sees using a concept that pertains to that aspect. Plautus may think: "I saw the back of Brutus as he was stabbing Caesar."

But this thought is subsequent to and is based upon his perception and is not an essential constituent of his visual experience. The fact that in order to see things we must see certain of their spatial aspects rather than others is no reason for thinking that perception incorporates any representational content whatever.

It may be thought that RTP would be better supported in those cases in which what is seen is determined not just by the geometry and physics of light rays but by the mental states of the perceiver. Take a familiar example of perceptual organization, such as the figure-ground phenomenon. In ordinary perception, things are usually seen as standing out against a background. I see the lamp on the table on which I am now writing as standing out against a white wall as a background. This figure-ground relationship does not apply to the lamp and the wall 'in themselves' but only as perceived. It is a phenomenal rather than a physical fact. It is a fact about how things appear rather than about how things really are.

We are not here concerned with the underlying physiological causes of the figure-ground phenomenon, but with whether it incorporates propositions or concepts or representations in its essential nature. We can easily tell that this form of perceptual organization is not controllable by one's conscious thoughts. No matter how I describe the lamp or the wall to myself, the lamp continues to stand out against the wall. The contrast between figure and ground is antecedent to thought and belief. We have no introspective evidence to support the view that it either consists of or is produced by our applying concepts to percepts. I know of no argument that shows that the contrast essentially exhibits either propositional or conceptual content. The state of affairs "lamp as standing out from wall" is something given and does not require to be thought in order to be given. Its being given is not an instance of any propositional attitude. The fact that the contrast is 'subjective' and is produced by the visual system is not sufficient to establish it as being representational.

There are examples of *seeing as* that, unlike the figure-ground contrast, can be controlled to some extent by our voluntary mental acts. Take Wittgenstein's well-known duck/rabbit example.[32] One looks at a picture that can be seen first *as* a duck and then *as* a rabbit. The same thing is seen *as* different things at different times. The duck/rabbit is an example of gestalt switch that is frequently described in the literature on the psychology of perception. The switch back and forth can be produced by staring at certain parts of the picture—to that extent it is under our control. The question is whether such cases of *seeing as* are representational or intentional in nature.

One must distinguish the switch from the duck to the rabbit from the accompanying thoughts, such as: "Now I see a duck, and now I see a rabbit." The thoughts are subsequent mental reports of the switch and are not constituents of it. It is because the picture now appears to be of a rabbit that I am prompted to think, "Now I see a rabbit." The switch is a change in the organization of the visual experience, not a change in my beliefs about what appears.

There is an empirical question whether or not only those who know what ducks and rabbits are can experience the switch. Is the activation of a concept causally necessary for the occurrence of a gestalt switch? Probably the answer is no, since one does not usually know (unless one is told ahead of time) which concepts would be relevant until the switch has occurred. But even if the answer is yes, this would only tell us that representations are causally necessary for certain perceptual phenomena, not that the phenomena themselves exemplify conceptual or propositional content.

In order for me to experience the gestalt switch as a switch from a duck to a rabbit, I must *know* that I am now seeing a duck and now seeing a rabbit. *Seeing as* in this sense does incorporate a representation. But the representation is a feature not of the visual appearance but of my immediate judgment that represents what this picture is a picture of. Logically it is possible that the switch occurs without my knowing that it is a switch from a duck to a rabbit. One may experience a switch in perceptual organization without conceptualizing it.

A statement made by one person about another, such as "Smith now sees it as a rabbit," is susceptible of two very different readings. According to the first, it says that the picture Smith is looking at is visually presented to Smith in its rabbit phase. According to the second, it says this but adds that Smith recognizes that it is a picture of a rabbit. The second, but not the first, entails the occurrence of a propositional attitude. But his recognition of it as a rabbit does not entail that his visual experience exemplifies propositional content. The content belongs to the recognition, which is a thought founded upon the visual appearance. With regard to the phenomenon of *seeing as* in general, in those cases in which it incorporates an intentional content, one will find that the content belongs to an associated propositional attitude rather than to the experience. Consequently, the phenomenon of *seeing as* does not tend to support RTP.

Searle's argument in behalf of the intentional character of perceptual consciousness is based upon two assumptions. The first is that an experience can be veridical or non-veridical; the second is that veridicality is or is analogous to truth, and non-veridicality is or is analogous to falsehood. It follows that in order to explain how an experience could be veridical or non-veridical, one must suppose that it exemplifies propositional content. But if we cannot find reason to accept RTP, then it is necessary to reexamine these assumptions.

A visual experience is veridical when there is a correspondence between appearance and reality. When something that is red looks red, then its looking red is veridical; when it looks red but is not red, then its looking red is non-veridical. The concept of veridicality is one that has frequent application, so the first assumption passes muster.

The second assumption attempts to explain what the appearance/reality correspondence consists of. According to RTP in Searle's version, it consists of the fact that its looking red truthfully represents the fact that it is red. If we reject RTP, then this assumption must be rejected as well. Is there some other account of veridicality that does not presuppose RTP?

When something that looks red is red, then it has the very *same* property that it looks to have. In veridical experience the items presented exist in just the way they are presented. To the extent that perceptual consciousness is veridical, the world, independently of perceptual consciousness, is disclosed as it is 'in itself'. A veridical experience is, as I earlier pointed out, correctly likened to an achievement; it shows how things are. A non-veridical experience constitutes a failure to disclose how things are; it presents the world in a way different from the way it is.

This identity theory of veridicality contrasts with the representational account of RTP. On the identity theory, representations enter into the picture not as essential constituents of perceptual consciousness but as subsequent judgments, based not only upon what experience presents but also upon background knowledge and belief, and capable of being true or false. Representations are interpretations of what perceptual consciousness appears to disclose. The identity theory is built into the conceptual scheme we use to characterize experiences and their relation to reality. We never suppose that when something is as it appears there is anything other than an identity between the apparent and the real character of the object.

The philosophical tradition from Descartes through Kant has argued in a variety of ways that sense perception is not a very reliable guide to how the world is in itself; sense perception even at its best fails to disclose accurately the nature of things-in-themselves; we cannot trust our senses very far. In the previous chapters I have endorsed this assessment of our cognitive predicament. In terms of the identity theory of veridicality, this assessment implies that sense perception fails to be veridical to a significant extent. Although objects appear to have colors, none of them really do. Things-in-themselves are bereft of color and perhaps of other secondary qualities. Indeed, nothing is colored.

An advocate of RTP may argue, finally, that even the identity theory of veridicality requires a representational account of sense experience. Consider some particular non-veridical experience— something that is not blue looks blue. How does it happen that the experience is as of blue? The experience itself does not have the color; nor does the object. How does blue enter the picture at all? RTP answers that blue enters the picture by being one of the qualities represented by the experience. The introduction of the semantic relation of mental representation here is the best explanation of how it is possible for the experience to be as of blue,[33] and since, with regard to its intra-somatic neural conditions, veridical experience comes about by the same processes as the non-veridical, the same explanation applies here as well.

When I am merely thinking of the blue color of some object, it is plausible to claim that the way that blue gets into my thought is by way of mental representation. The theory that thoughts are analogues of sentences is one of the more plausible theories of the nature of thinking and is directly supported by introspection, which frequently reveals sentence tokens of natural language to be what we are thinking in. But when a blue object is seen, its color is visually presented. Even if, as RTP claims, the sense experience represents the color, more than representation is required to explain the difference between thought and visual consciousness. What is distinctive of visual consciousness is that color is presented to a subject. But if we need to introduce presentational immediacy to demarcate visual consciousness from thought, then the representational hypothesis becomes superfluous. It is presentational immediacy that is doing all the work.

SEVEN

Subjectivism

According to Locke's pure power analysis and Reid's microstate theory, colors and other secondary qualities are objective features of bodies; color terms are true of bodies. In Locke's theory, the objectivity is qualified by reference to the fact that secondary qualities are identified by the effects that bodies produce upon perceivers. In both theories color terms also occur in appearance statements. This subjective aspect—apparent color—is the effect of real color.

Subjectivism is the view that real color and apparent color coincide. The objective features that the other accounts consider to be what colors really are, are considered by subjectivism to be the causes of colors, not the colors themselves.

Although subjectivism contradicts our common sense view of the matter, it can be shown to be the outcome of a plausible line of reasoning. The subjectivist insists that colors are the very items that appear or are directly given in visual experience. In this respect, there is agreement with common sense. To the common sense view, the subjectivist adds the scientific story of how color perception comes about and concludes that there is no room in the story for colors objectively considered. We have no reason to believe that the items given in visual experience are indeed exemplified in physical nature. They drop out of the physical picture entirely. But convinced beyond doubt that something has color, the subjectivist argues by elimination that color belongs to consciousness, to the mind rather than to nature. To use an older terminology, secondary qualities are ideas in the mind. As Berkeley said, they exist only insofar as they are perceived. Colors belong to our apprehensions of and responses to bodies, not to the bodies themselves. They are our subjective reactions to impinging energies, not objective features of corporeal things. Color and apparent color are the same. If, indeed, we apply color terms to bodies, that is an error caused by our projection and objectification of a mental item on nature, or, perhaps, it is a secondary and derivative use of terms in which they are, confusingly, applied to the causes of color as well as to the colors themselves.

But how can colors reside in consciousness? How can a mental or a brain event exemplify a color? If colors are in consciousness, it is not by way of exemplification. But what is the alternative? A way out of these difficulties was suggested by C. J. Ducasse, whose view has become known as the *adverbial theory of consciousness*:

> "Blue," "bitter," "sweet," etc., are names not of objects of experience, nor of species of objects of experience, but of *species of experience itself*. What this means is perhaps made clearest by saying that to sense blue is then to sense *bluely*, just as to dance the waltz is to dance "waltzily" (i.e. in the manner called "to waltz"). To jump a leap is to jump "leapily" (i.e. in the manner called "to leap"), etc. Sensing, that is to say, is a mental process

having to sensing blue the same logical relation which obtains, for example, between the process in a string called "vibrating" and a particular mode in which it vibrates—say the middle-C mode. Obviously, it would similarly be appropriate to say of the string that it is vibrating middle-C-ly. Sensing blue, I hold, is thus a species or modulation of sensing.[1]

The main points of the adverbial theory can be summed up as follows. First, in language, adverbs typically represent characteristics of events and changes. In "John is running swiftly," the adverb indicates a feature of John's running; it tells us how fast John runs. A characteristic of an event will be called an *adverbial property,* where the term "property" is broadly construed. In the second place, adverbial properties are occasionally represented by terms other than adverbs, as in "John is dancing a waltz." Here the noun "waltz" does not name an independently existing object but rather represents a particular pattern in which the dancer dances.

In the third place, according to the adverbial theory, language can be occasionally misleading about the category of the items it represents. If, in answer to the question "What color do you see?" John answers, "I see blue," one cannot conclude that just because "blue" is a noun, the item it names is an object of sight existing independently of the seeing of it. In the fourth place, we are, therefore, free to claim that the blue that is seen must somehow exist in consciousness, for there is no room for it in nature. But, in the fifth place, the only way to make sense of this fact is to suppose that blue is an adverbial property of the visual experience in which it appears. So it is reasonable to suppose that the ontological structure of the event-type represented by "Something looks blue to X" is more perspicuously rendered by "X is sensing something bluely."

In the sixth place, it would be a mistake to infer that because blue is an adverbial property of a visual experience, the experience is blue in the sense that it exemplifies the color blue in the way that a blue surface exemplifies blue. Rather, the adverbial properties named by secondary quality terms constitute the species or type of event. Thus "'bitter' is the name of the gustatory quality which the given taste *is,* not of a property which the taste *has.*"[2] Secondary qualities are types of experiences. Among the adverbial properties are those that we may call *adverbial types,* among which are the secondary qualities.

We are now in a position to recognize that the adverbial theory models secondary quality experiences on the structure of bodily sensations. When I feel a toothache, for example, I cannot suppose that the ache exists independently of my awareness of it. The ache pervades the awareness; it is one with the feeling of it. The adverbial theory provides a plausible account of this unity of the feeling with the felt object. In the same way, it insists upon a unity of perceived secondary qualities with the experience of them. Blue is related to my experience of blue just as my toothache is related to my feeling of it. One advantage of the adverbial theory for a subjectivist view of colors is that unlike the alternative sense-datum approach, it can provide a plausible explanation of why colors exist only as perceived. The dependence of color upon the perception of it is incorporated into its very ontological structure.

Although the adverbial theory is frequently presented as part of an account of secondary qualities, it cannot, logically, be confined within just those borders. As a theory of what it means for a secondary quality to be 'in' consciousness, it takes its start from the fact that such qualities *appear* in sense perception; they are among the items that are immediately and directly presented via perceptual consciousness. That they appear is the starting point of discussion. But, as Berkeley has pointed out, primary qualities are on a par with the secondary as far as the appearances go. An object may appear to have a shape as well as a color; it may appear to have a shape that it does not really have. Moreover, color and shape are 'blended' together in perception. The extent of apparent color determines the apparent shape.[3] So we have the same reason to treat apparent shape and the other primary qualities as adverbial types as we have to treat colors in this way. Although this extension of the adverbial theory no doubt complicates it, it has the advantage of presenting the theory as a general account of the 'contents' of consciousness rather than just an *ad hoc* device for dealing with the secondary qualities.

One way of interpreting the theory is to take it as an account of the semantics of secondary and primary quality terms as they occur in ordinary non-technical discourse. But so understood, it has an implication that is mistaken. For it implies that these terms differ in meaning when describing appearances and when describing bodies. When I say, "This looks blue and square," the terms "blue" and "square" are to be interpreted as representing adverbial types of conscious experiences. But when I say of the same thing, "This is blue and square," these terms must be understood differently. Exactly how they are to be interpreted will depend upon how sensible qualities, objectively taken, are to be construed. But however construed, they will not be understood as properties of conscious experiences.

But we saw earlier that there is no such semantic duality. When I say of something that is blue and square that it looks blue and square, then it really does have the very same qualities that it also looks to have. The qualities that are introduced in ordinary appearance talk are no different in nature from those objectively predicated of bodies. That apparent qualities are adverbial types of conscious experiences is a view that cannot be extracted from the meaning of our ordinary appearance locutions.

These locutions are not analogous, in respect to meaning, to type words for bodily sensations. Terms such as "toothache," "tickle," and "tingle" can be interpreted as names of feelings and thus as classifications of conscious experiences. But there is no exactly parallel interpretation for "blue" or for "bitter." When something that is bitter tastes bitter as well, then the way it tastes is identical to the way it is. In the case of bitter, however, in contrast to blue, there is a corresponding bodily sensation, so the adverbial theory may, perhaps, apply to one aspect of a gustatory experience. We can even say, "I have a bitter taste in my mouth," where "bitter" here is extended beyond its standard application to things that may be tasted to the sensation caused by such things. What is said here is that I have a sensation in my mouth that is characteristic of the sensations I usually obtain when I taste bitter things. The sensation is characterized indirectly via reference to the typical causes of sensations of that type. But in vision there are no bodily sensations, so there is no opening for an adverbial interpretation of "blue" as there is for "bitter."

Instead of interpreting the adverbial theory as an account of our ordinary meanings and of the common sense of the matter, we might more plausibly render it as the outcome of a different story. Suppose we start out with the view of Hobbes and Locke that our ordinary use of color terms is profoundly in error. It is just a mistake to impute, as we do, apparent colors to bodies, for they are actually properties of conscious experiences. We are endowed with a mental mechanism by means of which we unconsciously 'project' colors upon bodies and regions of space.

According to Wilfrid Sellars, "In visual perception we mistake our sensory states for features of physical objects."[4] Colors are not presented to us as they really are. "The volume of pink of which we are aware does not present itself as a sensory state of ourselves —even though . . . that is what it turns out to be."[5] We *discover* that that is what it turns out to be when the scientific theory of perception makes use of colors *qua* states of perceivers in explaining visual perception. "When the larger story is in, expanses of color in the environment turn out to be miscategorized states of perceivers."[6]

According to Sellars, the scientific story recategorizes colors as sensory states of perceivers. As a result, it clashes with the categorization of the common sense picture, and when there is a clash between science and common sense, so much the worse for common sense. Thus the adverbial theory of color terms, according to this reading, is neither an analysis of ordinary usage nor a technical equivalent of it, but a theoretical proposal of science intended to correct the error about color caused, in Hobbes's words, by "the great deception of sense."

An initial difficulty with this approach is based upon the need to treat color and shape similarly. We saw that apparent shape should be treated as an adverbial type if apparent color is. But it is implausible to suppose that real shapes, shapes as exemplified by bodies, turn out in the scientific story to be adverbial types. Why then should we agree with Sellars that colors turn out to be adverbial types? If we can resist the pressure toward recategorization in the case of shape, should we not do so as well in the case of color?

Of course, there is an important difference between shape and color, all things considered. In the Lockean argument, shapes objectively considered are indispensable components of the picture of nature that science constructs to explain sense perception and many other phenomena. But colors, objectively considered, drop out of the picture. They play no explanatory role. Shapes have a fixed place, but colors do not. There is a temptation to find a place for colors as well. Identifying them with sensory states of perceivers seems to be the best that can be done to 'save' the phenomena. But why try to save the phenomena? If colors drop out of the picture, why not just leave them out permanently? Why should they be permitted to creep back into the picture at all?

Quite a while ago, demons dropped out of the picture in our explanations of illness. We do not try to keep them in the picture by recategorizing them. We do not say that demons are really germs. Why not let colors go the way of demons? There is this difference between demons and colors. It is relatively easy (for us post-Enlightenment intellectuals) to give up the belief in demons, but no matter how hard I try, I cannot give up the belief that, for example, the pen with which I am writing this sentence is black. Enlightened as I am, I am nevertheless stuck with colors. And everyone else is in the same boat.

I shall consider the problem of our belief in color in the next chapter. Here, all that needs to be said is that we can explain the difference between colors and demons in this respect by pointing out that our unavoidable belief in the reality of color is caused by the way our visual apparatus works, and if we are lucky, that apparatus is a permanent component of our nervous system. Our belief in demons, however, is not entrenched in our psyche by some permanent neural apparatus, so we can easily discard it. This explanation of the difference does not bring color back into the picture. So the difference with respect to belief no more justifies our attempting to find a place for colors than it would justify our attempting to find one for demons.

The error that Sellars attributes to our common sense framework of taking what are really adverbial types to be objective features of bodies is so peculiar that it is difficult to believe that it can occur. It is an error that consists in taking something that is not extended or shaped and presenting it to ourselves as something inextricably bound up with an objective spatial order. What makes us think that that very thing 'disguised' as an inextricable spatial item is identical to something that in its true nature is just a sensory state? It is as if numbers always came disguised as smells. How can there be a disguise that good?

Although the adverbial account of color fails in both its scientific and its common sense interpretations, there is still a genuine problem that needs to be addressed. It is the problem of giving an account of the ontological structure of experiences in which colors appear. Suppose I am in a situation in which something looks blue to me and that the thing that appears is not really blue. So there is no blue there that anything exemplifies or possesses at all, according to the argument I have presented so far. But then how does it come about that this experience is one in which something looks *blue*? How does the concept of blue get into the picture at all as I describe my experience?

A plausible answer is that the experience resembles the experience I characteristically have when I see something that is blue. I note the resemblance and describe my experience in terms of "looks blue." But what exactly is the resemblance that I have noticed? Remember that two experiences are involved:

(1) I see something that is blue, and it appears blue.
(2) I do not see anything blue, but something looks blue.

According to (1) but not (2), blue is actually exemplified as well as perceptually presented. So (1) and (2) are not alike with respect to the givenness of actual blue. They do resemble one another as being cases of visual consciousness, but that is not the relevant similarity, since in that respect they are also similar to:

(3) I see something that is red, and it appears red.

The relevant similarity is that both (1) and (2) describe an experience that has the property of *blue's appearing*. This property is the same in both cases. But this leaves the problem of determining the structure of the property. After all, the color blue is not an exemplified constituent of it, for if it were, (2) would collapse into (1). But if blue is not an exemplified constituent, and if red is not an exemplified constituent of *red's appearing*, the property implicated in (3), then how do (1) and (2) differ from (3)? How does *blue's appearing* differ from *red's appearing*?

Enter sense data. These are supposed to be mental particulars that actually exemplify the qualities that bodies appear to have. They were introduced in many theories of perception as inner representations of external realities. In such accounts, perceptual experiences are interpreted as consisting of a direct awareness of a sense datum or of a complex of sense data. The visual field of an individual at a moment of time is taken as an array of sense data. Sense-datum theories lost their popularity about a generation ago as more and more philosophers opted for a materialistic ontology in which there is no room for sense data. But whatever their metaphysical deficiencies, sense data at least could be used to answer our question. *Blue's appearing* differs from *red's appearing* in that the former is an awareness of a blue sense datum, whereas the latter is an awareness of a red one. We are able to preserve the difference between (1) and (2); according to (1), one sees a blue material object via being aware of a blue sense datum, whereas in (2), one is just aware of the sense datum. The sense-datum theory is thus an alternative to the adverbial account in providing us with a subjectivist view of secondary qualities. This version of subjectivism says that sense data and only sense data exemplify apparent secondary qualities. For this reason, I shall consider it briefly in this chapter.

According to the sense-datum approach, a blue particular actually is a constituent of *blue's appearing*. The theory offers an explanation of the structure of appearance in terms of the exemplification by mental entities of qualities that appear. That a visual experience has the property of *blue's appearing* consists of the individual whose experience it is being aware of a blue sense datum.

The main traditional argument in favor of the sense-datum approach has been based upon Cartesian appeals to the indubitable. Consider this well-known passage by H. H. Price:

When I see a tomato there is much that I can doubt. I can doubt whether it is a tomato that I am seeing, and not a cleverly painted piece of wax. I can doubt whether there is any material thing there at all. Perhaps what I took for a tomato was really a reflection; perhaps I am even the victim of some hallucination. One thing however I cannot doubt: that there exists a red patch of a round and somewhat bulgy shape, standing out from a background of other colour patches, and having a certain visual depth, and that this whole field of colour is directly present to my consciousness.[7]

The method illustrated in this passage consists of a perceiver's identifying the things that he could be mistaken about given the experiences he is then and there having. The items whose existence he can doubt are then bracketed and put aside. Sense data enter the picture as items whose existence and qualities cannot be doubted. They are the indubitable residues of the Cartesian procedure. "There is something red there; that I cannot doubt," asserts Price.

Consider a holograph image of Price's red tomato. This is a three-dimensional image that can be produced by a special form of laser photography. It is very lifelike, so that one can almost believe that one is seeing the real thing. When I look at the photographic plate, I see an image that looks exactly like a red tomato. I know very well that there is no tomato there at all, and I know that neither the photographic plate nor any other physical object in my field of vision is red. But can I doubt that there is something red of which I am conscious?

Having introduced sense data by the method of doubt, we need a further argument to establish that the holographic image is a mental particular. We know that one can become aware of the image only when one's visual apparatus is stimulated by a beam of light reflected from the photographic plate. When the stimulus ceases, not only does the awareness of the image cease, but the image itself no longer exists. There is no reason at all to suppose that it continues to exist unperceived. The image is something mental in the sense that its existence depends upon our consciousness of it.

Price's argument does not have the logical force of Descartes's

Cogito argument. Descartes was able to prove that he himself exists on the grounds that his very attempt to doubt his existence implies or presupposes that he exists. This is a *strong* indubitability argument, according to which the existence of the very fact whose reality one is attempting to doubt is logically implied by one's attempting to doubt it. Price's argument is at best a *weak* indubitability argument because the existence of the red patch is not entailed by the perceiver's attempt to doubt it. From the fact that it looks to a perceiver as if she is seeing something red and from the fact that she cannot rid herself of the belief that there is something red there, it does not follow logically that her belief is true. So Price's argument fails to be logically conclusive. If it has any rational force at all, it consists in providing us with a less than conclusive reason for thinking that there are sense data. That there is something red there that is seen is attested to by the 'evidence' of the senses. Perceptual evidence is a reason for believing in the truth of certain propositions. We seldom have better reason for believing in the existence of certain states of affairs than that we are perceptually conscious of them.

Because the reason is not logically conclusive, it is logically possible that there are arguments against the belief in the red patch that outweigh and defeat the evidence of the senses. For instance, one reason against supposing that there really is a holograph tomato image that one is seeing is that there is no place for images in nature or mind.[8] Images just don't fit in. The attempt to make them fit in has encouraged theories of nature and mind that have nothing else to recommend them. Thus the evidence of the senses can be challenged by far-reaching metaphysical considerations.

If I am right in rejecting both the adverbial and the sense-datum accounts of the structure of appearance, how can we distinguish between *blue's appearing* and *red's appearing*? How can they be individuated without reinstating the very color qualities that we have found no room for in nature or mind? I will suggest two further possibilities. The first is that a feature of visual experience such as *blue's appearing* has aspects that are not introspectively discernible but that can differentiate it from *red's appearing*. This option seems to presuppose that we can successfully identify these features with brain states that have more to them than meets the introspective eye. But this option fails, I think, for reasons similar to those that defeated the dual-aspect version of the microstate theory of color. For if *blue's appearing* is a distinguishable aspect of a brain state, distinct from the state's other aspects, then reference to these other aspects fails to individuate it.

Another possibility, the one that I am inclined to favor, is to suppose that phenomenal qualities can be perceptually presented even though nothing exemplifies them. Our visual experience is a form of consciousness in the mode of "presentational immediacy";[9] its immediate content is presented rather than represented; and the description of its phenomenal content leaves open the question of which, if any, of its presented qualities are exemplified. *Blue's appearing* is to be distinguished from *red's appearing* on the grounds of the difference of presented quality. In the next chapter I shall make some additional remarks about this way of conceiving of the issue.

EIGHT

Color Skepticism

Earlier in this book I discussed Locke's argument that shows that secondary qualities cannot be real or occurrent qualities of bodies. We cannot reasonably suppose that colors are real qualities of bodies, because they play no active causal role in the scientific theories about nature that we use to explain the course of human experience. But we also had reason to reject Locke's alternative theory, the pure power analysis. In addition we were unable to find any reasons for accepting the main rivals to Locke's positive account. Neither the idea that colors are microstates of bodies nor the claim that they are actually exemplified constituents of consciousness was able to survive criticism. Each of the rejected accounts has the same basic flaw; each characterizes color in a way that fails to capture its true nature. Each must deny our common understanding of the sort of quality color is. In its account of color, each changes the subject.

We are now apparently at an impasse. For if colors are neither pure powers nor microstates nor features of consciousness, what else is there for them to be? The scientific theories that provide the best explanations of physical and mental phenomena seem to provide no other plausible candidates. Given the nature of color, nothing whose existence our theories warrant can plausibly be identified with color.

The best reason for favoring one or another of these rejected accounts of color is that each of them can be so interpreted that most of the judgments that we make about objects and their colors that we think are true turn out to be true. At this very moment, for example, I am firmly convinced that the surface of the table on which I am writing these words is white. That belief of mine comes out true on each account. Even subjectivism can interpret this belief so that "That is white" can be understood as a statement about the causes of apparent color. However, as we have seen, none of our affirmative color judgments is indubitable in a way that endows this reason with a force that outweighs any other possible consideration. In fact, the weight of the argument as it has developed up to this point leads us to the following skeptical outcome: nothing has any color; none of the judgments in which we ascribe a color to something are true. Nothing exists that has color, although our nature constrains us to believe the contrary. Nature causes us to believe in color because colors are caused to appear in the visual experiences of everyone capable of seeing. The experience of color pervades our conscious life. Yet Locke's argument as well as the facts of contemporary color science[1] show us that bodies would appear just as they do appear even if nothing had any color at all. So the fact that bodies look as if they exemplify colors provides no solid support for thinking that they really do so.

One argument that may be thought to be unfavorable to this color skepticism is the view that colors in fact function frequently as causes, and that there are even laws of color.[2] However, many of the causal relations that initially seem to be good candidates for laws of color are really connections among some of the following: microstates of bodies, light waves, and visual experiences, none of which, I have argued, presuppose the existence of color. Take, for example, the claim that my seeing something as red causes me to believe that it is red. Doesn't the shade of red that I see play a causal role in the generation of my belief? The answer is no. What directly causes my belief is the fact that the thing I see looks red to me; and what causes it to look red is a constellation of physical conditions none of which includes color as a constituent. But what about aesthetic experience? I look at a painting, and as a result of seeing a medley of colors, certain emotions arise in me. Don't the perceived colors play a role in the emergence of the emotion? Again the answer is no. The emotion is directly caused by the visual experience in which certain colors are presented, but this can occur even if nothing exemplifies color. As a general rule, when tempted to ascribe a causal role to color, consider instead whether the bearers of such agency are not really certain visual experiences or physical states.

Another apparent difficulty with color skepticism is that our color predicates have meaning and that we learn their meaning by pointing to examples of color. H. H. Price makes this point in the course of arguing in behalf of sense data:

When something looks φ in this literal, and visual sense of the word, there is no denying that the word 'looks' comes very close to being a kind of 'is'. . . . When something looks φ, we are provided with an ostensive definition of the concept φ. Does it not follow from this that we are aware of a φ-ish particular, an entity that does actually exemplify or instantiate the character ϕ? And that is very like the sense-datum philosopher's way of treating appearing verbs.[3]

An ostensive definition of a term is, according to Price's account, one that explains its meaning by providing an actual instance of it. In order to provide someone with an ostensive definition of, for example, "camel," one must show him a camel. Price claims that since something's looking red provides an occasion for giving an ostensive definition of "red," then in something's looking red, something must actually be red. The argument is intended to establish that if colors appear, then in the appearances there must exist instances of color exemplification.

An initial difficulty with Price's argument as stated is that it has obvious counter-examples. One could, for example, teach someone the meaning of "unicorn" by providing him with a visual image of one—say by showing him a picture. It certainly does not follow that unicorns exist. Perhaps Price might reply that his argument applies to what Locke called simple ideas rather than complex concepts. We can form complex concepts of non-entities by arranging in our minds concepts and images of their constituents. But simple concepts, such as color concepts,[4] must be notions of what exists; they cannot be formed by an arrangement of their constituents, for they have none.

Suppose that nothing has any color. Then given Price's explanation of what an ostensive definition is, it follows that we cannot provide ostensive definitions of color terms. But it does not follow that we cannot explain their meaning by reference to the appearances. For when something looks red, I am able to form an idea or concept of something that would be a color if it were exemplified. In the case of colors, their apparent existence is a sufficient basis for explaining the meanings of their names. Even if colors were exemplified by bodies, it would still be by their appearances that we would acquire our conceptions of them. So if colors are not exemplified, we are in as good a position as we would be if they were to endow our color terms with meaning.

For the most part, I have formulated color skepticism as the claim that nothing exemplifies or has any color. Another possible formulation is that colors do not exist, that there is no such thing as color. However, these formulations are not equivalent, for although the latter entails the former, the former does not entail the latter. With respect to a universal, to an entity that is capable of being exemplified, it is one thing to say that nothing exemplifies it and another to say that there is no such thing. To a Platonist, who subscribes to a thesis often ascribed to Plato that the Forms exist independently of the particulars that participate in them, colors may very well exist even if all the arguments favorable to color skepticism are correct.

The issues raised by Platonism are weighty and cannot be settled here. I shall adopt the first formulation of color skepticism as the official version, and none of the arguments in its favor either presuppose or deny the stronger Platonic version. The problem of universals is mostly a side show with respect to the question of color skepticism. However, I shall mention several considerations that may be thought to be pertinent.

There is an argument for an Aristotelian conception of universals according to which a universal exists only insofar as it is exemplified or has actual instances. Notice how we speak of the biological species or types that have played a role in the theory of evolution. We speak of certain species as having come into existence and others as being endangered or as going out of existence entirely. We develop theories about how the various species came into existence in the first place. Our talk about species suggests that the existence of the type is tied to its having members. It seems absurd to say that even if all tigers should disappear from the face of the earth, nevertheless the tiger species would still exist.

However, even if we buy this argument as far as biological types are concerned, there are two considerations that should make us more sympathetic to a Platonic conception of colors. In the first place, there are truths about colors that hold independent of their exemplification. For example, that orange is more like red than it is like green does not seem to entail that anything is orange or red or green. Of course, we would not be in a position to grasp truths about color resemblances unless colors appeared to us, but even color appearances do not entail that anything is orange or red or green. If there are such truths, then it seems that there is a subject matter for them to be about.

Second, I argued in the previous chapter that even though nothing has a color, colors are perceptually presented and, as presented, serve to individuate visual experiences and to distinguish them from one another. It is puzzling to think that a total non-entity can play this role. Earlier in this century, the critical realists argued that "the datum is a mere essence, a universal," and explained that "error in perception . . . is possible only because the givenness of the essence is independent of its embodiment."[5] Visual perception is non-veridical to a great extent because the colors that are given are not embodied as we normally believe them to be. The cost of avoiding the sense-datum theory while taking visual experience seriously seems to be that we are committed to a Platonic account of qualities that are perceptually presented.

Some philosophers prefer nominalism with respect to colors.[6] They claim that in all truths that employ color terms, the terms occur as predicates, never in referential position, and that, therefore, the assertion of such truths never commits us to the existence of color. They claim, then, that color terms need never be used to refer to colors. However, they admit that color terms as predicates are true of or are false of various material objects. For philosophers who take such a stand, color skepticism can be formulated as the claim that color predicates are never true of any objects.

There is another, apparently insurmountable, difficulty for color skepticism. One of the steps in Locke's argument that has been used to support the skeptical position is to appeal to scientific theories of color and light to determine which features of bodies are responsible for our color perceptions. But these theories are empirical; the evidence in their favor includes a large body of observational data. Much of the data consists of reports of what has been seen by investigators and experimental subjects; the perception of color is an inextricable component of what we see. But color skepticism says that we do not actually see colors, although we think we do. So the observational data are illusory and substantially non-veridical, and the reports based upon them are shot full of error. Thus the conclusion of the skeptical argument—that nothing exemplifies color and that visual perception is quite unreliable—falsifies some of its premises. The argument, it would appear, is self-defeating and self-refuting.

This criticism possesses the following logical structure. On the basis of a theory T plus other considerations, a conclusion C has been drawn. T is based upon evidence E. But C implies that E

is untrustworthy. Thus according to C, one has no right to rely upon T in order to justify C. So C undermines its own apparent justification.

This difficulty is not, however, fatal to color skepticism. Occasionally, a theory T and the implications drawn from it may require that the evidence on which it is based be reconsidered. It may turn out that there are numerous falsehoods among the evidence statements E. It is possible that T has succeeded in refuting itself. But there is another possibility. Perhaps the false statements in E can be purged of that part of their content that is responsible for their being false and be reformulated so as to be true and to continue to support T.

In the case at hand, suppose that among the evidence statements E for the scientific component T of Locke's argument, there are statements that imply that colors are exemplified by bodies. According to C—which says that colors are never exemplified by anything—these statements are false. Let us suppose, to simplify matters, that each of these false statements is of the form "X is F," where X refers to a body and F represents a color. However, corresponding to each false statement, there is a true one of the form "X appears to exemplify F" or "X looks F." In the light of what T says about the causal interactions between the microstates of bodies, light, and the human visual apparatus, these appearance statements can replace their false counterparts in E and can support T as well as their counterparts did. So we can replace E with an emended set of evidence statements that are not falsified by C. Thus color skepticism is not inherently self-refuting.

Among the beliefs that are produced by perceptual experience, some are natural and some are instructed. A natural perceptual belief is one that we form uninfluenced by scientific or technical knowledge. Our instructed beliefs include those natural beliefs that have survived criticism in the light of our current science as well as corrections of those of our natural beliefs that have failed the critical test. The reason that color skepticism is not self-refuting is that although it implies that some of the natural beliefs that support it are false, there is a corresponding set of instructed beliefs that are true and that support it just as well.

According to color skepticism, the world as it exists 'in itself', independently of our visual and other perceptual experience, is vastly different from the world as it appears. Inherent in all human visual perception (and perhaps in other forms of sense perception as well) is a pervasive illusion. The illusion does not consist in our unconsciously 'projecting' color qualities onto objects that fail to exemplify them, for there are no exemplified qualities to project. Rather, it consists in the fact that our visual experiences are not veridical with respect to color and that we are caused to believe what is false, namely that bodies do exemplify color.

Most of those who take Locke's arguments seriously, however, have been unwilling to go so far as to be skeptics about color. For example, here is how Putnam 'saves' the appearances:

Vision does not give us direct access to a ready-made world, but gives us a description of objects which are partly structured and constituted by vision itself. If we take the physicist's rainbow to be the rainbow 'in itself', then the rainbow 'in itself' has no *bands* (a spectroscopic analysis yields a smooth distribution of frequencies); the red, orange, yellow, green, blue, and violet bands are a feature of the perceptual rainbow, not the physicist's rainbow. The perceptual rainbow depends on the nature of our perceptual apparatus itself. . . . Yet we do not consider vision as defective because it sees bands in the rainbow; someone who couldn't see them would have defective vision. Vision is certified as good by its ability to deliver a description which fits the object *for us,* not metaphysical things in themselves. Vision is good when it enables us to see the world 'as it is'—that is, the human functional world which is partly created by vision itself.[7]

In order to avoid imputing error to vision, Putnam distinguishes objects as they are for us and metaphysical things-in-themselves. Objects as they are for us constitute the human functional world, which, he claims, is, in part, constituted by our human visual apparatus.

Objects as they are for humans generally consist of objects as they appear in sense perception insofar as we discount individual peculiarities and consider only normal cases. That this human functional world is partly created by vision is true in the sense that how things look generally to human beings may differ markedly from how they look to other species and that these differences can be explained by reference to differences in the visual apparatus of different species.

However, the contrast that Putnam relies upon between objects for us and metaphysical things-in-themselves is not the one that is pertinent for our problem. If metaphysical things-in-themselves are interpreted à la Kant as unknowable entities, then they drop out of the picture as far as we are concerned. There is nothing to be said about them. But that does not mean that we are left only with the human functional world. The physicist's rainbow is neither a metaphysical thing-in-itself nor an item in the human functional world. It belongs to the world as comprehended by scientific inquiry. And that world is just as much a world for us as is the human functional world or the world as it appears. The world comprehended by science is the world in which we exist and whose laws govern our transactions with objects. One of the tasks of science is to contribute to an objective view of *our* world, a view that discounts the peculiarities of various cognitive agents and does not mistake the features that are imputed to objects as a result of these peculiarities for features that objects actually exemplify. For example, one person sees spots before his eyes; according to his personal view, the world is spotty. But the community of cognitive agents does not, as a whole, confirm that the world is spotty. So his perceptions are peculiar to him, and are judged to be erroneous when we wish to know how things really stand.

What Putnam calls the human functional world is objective only in a limited way, namely relative to humans with normal perceptions; the peculiarities of abnormal perceivers are discounted. However, we have learned from everyday observation as well as from the study of the biological structures that underlie perception that peculiarities in the views of cognitive agents pertain not only to individuals but to species. Different species of animals perceive the world quite differently; some see things in black and white and others in color; some see different ranges of color or hear different ranges of sound from others. A peculiarity is species-wide when some feature is imputed to objects by normal cognitive agents within the species that the objects fail to exemplify. A species-wide peculiarity that is perceptual is an imputation grounded upon a non-veridical experience; in such cases, the perceptual apparatus of the species is delivering incorrect information. Such misinformation may, nevertheless, be useful when it is correlated to real features of things. In any case, a species-wide peculiarity of perception constitutes a lack of objectivity, a failure to grasp the knowable world as it really is. Metaphysical things-in-themselves play no role whatever in this account of the nature of objectivity.

How objective is the human functional world? This question cannot be answered *a priori. A priori,* there is no better reason to consider it to be a more accurate rendition of reality than the functional worlds of dogs or bats. We *discover* that the rainbow as it appears is non-veridical by comparing it, as does Putnam, with the rainbow as understood by physics, that is, with the rainbow objectively considered. Simply stated, the rainbow has no bands, although it appears to have them. We also *discover* that human visual perception in general is non-veridical with respect to color; that is what color skepticism asserts. And that implies that our vision, even our normal vision, is defective because it causes us to acquire numerous false beliefs.

Of course, we are 'programmed' to favor the human functional world. It constitutes the system of perceptions with which we must cope. But the fact that we make successful use of it on a practical, everyday level no more proves that it is free from error than the fact that dogs do very well with their system establishes its freedom from error. One of the achievements of the objective view that we have already attained is that we can explain how the human visual apparatus is useful in the concerns of daily life despite the fact that much of the information that it delivers is erroneous. So its utility does not prove its veridicality.

There is a certain argument that is suggested by Putnam when he says, "We do not consider vision as defective because it sees bands in the rainbow; someone who couldn't see them would have defective vision." It can be formulated in this way. There is a broad human consensus with respect to our perceptions and our perceptual judgments. If you see something as green, others will likely see it as green as well. There is widespread agreement in our judgments about colors, and this serves as evidence for widespread similarities in our visual experiences. Occasionally, someone will make a judgment or report a perception that disagrees with the consensus. He will, for example, see something as brown when almost everyone else sees it as red. Upon investigation, we find that he suffers from a form of color blindness and that his visual apparatus is abnormal. He suffers from an illusion; the rest of us do not; his vision is defective; ours is veridical.

According to this appeal to the consensus, there is no better reason for thinking that a person's experiences of and beliefs about color are correct than that they agree with the experiences and beliefs of others. The consensus is the test of veridicality. If someone disagrees, she is likely to be in error. If the disagreement can be explained by reference to the way her visual apparatus differs either permanently or temporarily from most people's, then it is even more likely that she is mistaken. This theory of the criterion of perceptual truth implies that our perceptual judgments *en masse* cannot reasonably be criticized on the basis of our scientific discoveries about the causes of perception. What science tells us cannot require us to revise our common sense perceptual beliefs insofar as they fit in with the human consensus.

This argument is only superficially persuasive and is fundamentally mistaken. In the first place, when I claim, for example, that my judgment that this is green is correct or true, I do not mean or imply that others agree with me about it. The concept of agreement or consensus is not a constituent of the concept of truth. Indeed, the view that it is, is incoherent. Suppose we both assert that it is true that this is green. Then you imply that you agree with me.

113

But about what? About the fact that I agree with you? What we agree about is that this is green, a purported state of affairs that, if it obtains, does so quite independently of our judgments and agreements.

There is this much truth in the argument from consensus: the fact that others agree with me increases my confidence in the truth of what I assert. But the increase in confidence is not a consequence of any conceptual connection between truth and agreement, but is based upon my background assumptions about the reliability of other people's cognitive apparatus. Such assumptions are contingent, fallible, and uncertain. The illusion of certainty is a product of our instinctive reliance upon our natural uninstructed beliefs rather than upon any reflective account of the basis of human knowledge. We can begin to bring home to ourselves their uncertainty by recalling established facts about divergences in perception among species. We may then come to realize that some degree of correspondence, rather than precise veridicality, is sufficient for the utility of visual perception in sustaining life and furthering our goals. Such doubts about the reliability of the human perceptual system that are thus engendered are not just Cartesian logical possibilities but serve to stimulate real doubts about the objective validity of the human consensus.

Color skepticism provides us with a specific set of reasons, founded upon the results of the various sciences concerned with color and perception, for doubting the human consensus as far as some of the secondary qualities are concerned. If the human perceptual consensus is unreliable to the extent that I have argued, then we all share in a collective hallucination. By a hallucination, I mean a perceptual experience that seems to present us with an object or state of affairs or quality that does not exist or fails to obtain or to be exemplified. All visual perception presents us with colors and colored objects, although in fact nothing at all exemplifies color. So all visual perception includes a hallucinatory phase, and since we all share in it, the hallucination is collective.

There is nothing absurd or unintelligible in the idea of a collective hallucination. For what makes a set of experiences hallucinatory is not that it disagrees with the established consensus, but that it disagrees with the way things are. A specific consensus may be a reliable sign of the way things are, provided that the explanation of how it came about implies that it is veridical or correct. But arguments may be offered, as in the case of color, to show that the way it came about has no tendency at all to support the claim that it is reliable.

One reason that may be offered against the idea that our color perceptions are collective hallucinations is that the application of the concept of a hallucination depends upon a contrast between veridical and hallucinatory experience.[8] We understand how Macbeth's experience of a dagger can be hallucinatory because we know what it would be like to have a veridical experience of a dagger. But according to color skepticism, no such contrast applies in the case of color. Since all of our color perceptions are hallucinatory, we have no conception at all of what a veridical color perception would be like. If there were a veridical color perception, it would be no different at all from one that is hallucinatory. Moreover, in daily life, it is argued, we are able to distinguish between perceptions that are veridical and those that are not. Occasionally, an object appears to have a color different from its real color. In such cases, we have established ways of identifying the delusion and of discovering the real color. But if no such contrast can be drawn, the very concept of a hallucination is empty.

As stated, this argument may be interpreted as making one or another of the following claims. (A) It may be saying that if the contrast cannot be drawn within experience, then one can never know whether or not an experience is veridical. In that case, there would be no evidence in favor of there being a collective hallucination. (B) Or, more strongly, it may be claiming that if the contrast cannot be drawn, the very idea of a hallucination is unintelligible.

In response to (A), if our experiences were all that we had to rely upon, then it would be true that without a contrast within experience, we would not be able to tell which experiences are veridical and which are not. But we are not as limited as (A) supposes. For we can also make use of our scientific theories, which hypothesize what the world is like independent of our experiences, in order to determine the reliability of any individual experience or group of them. It is true that these theories rest upon experience for their confirmation, but there is no inextricable problem of self-refutation or self-undermining, as we have seen.

In response to (B), the absence of the relevant contrast in color perception is no permanent bar to our developing the idea of a perceptual hallucination and applying it to color perception. For such contrasts may be found with respect to other sensible qualities such as shape. Illusions of shape that can be identified without recourse to recondite theories of the nature of matter allow us to form the concept of a non-veridical experience and apply it to cases where the use of such theories cannot be avoided. Empirically identifiable perceptual mistakes provide us with the idea that experience can be the basis not only of information, but of misinformation as well, and enable us to distinguish, once we become reflective, our own personal points of view from an objective view to be produced by inquiry.

As a matter of common sense, we do in fact occasionally mark certain of our color experiences as non-veridical, in contrast to the vast majority that we think are veridical. We have well-established ways of telling the difference. Now, this contrast that belongs to everyday life is compatible with the claim that all color perceptions are hallucinatory. For that they are all hallucinatory is based upon the idea that nothing exemplifies color. But that some are veridical from the standpoint of everyday life is based upon the idea that some color appearances are normal and regular and occur under certain conditions of vision. Even if the argument of this chapter is accepted, there is no need to surrender the contrast that is so useful for ordinary purposes.

The argument against color skepticism based upon the human consensus is a kind of appeal to common sense. We all agree on something throughout the course of our lives, so there is no basis for doubting it. We saw, however, that there can be a basis for doubting what we can agree upon, so agreement fails to provide an incorrigible or even a reliable mark of truth.

G. E. Moore appealed to common sense in a different way in his well-known 'proof' of an external world. Although color skepticism is by no means the same sort of doubt as Descartes's skepticism about the external world in his *Meditations*, nevertheless it is tempting and not very difficult to apply Moore's 'proof' to the case at hand. In the remainder of this chapter, I shall explore the type of appeal to common sense that is characteristic of his philosophy.

Moore's 'proof' is contained in this passage:

It seems to me that, so far from its being true, as Kant declares to be his opinion, that there is only one possible proof of the existence of things outside us, namely the one which he has given, I can now give a large number of different proofs, each of which is a perfectly rigorous proof; and that at many other times I have been in a position to give many others. I can prove now, for instance, that two human hands exist. How? By holding up my two hands, and saying, as I make a certain gesture with the right hand, 'Here is one hand,' and adding, as I make a certain gesture with the left, 'and here is another.' And if, by doing this, I have proved *ipso facto,* the existence of external things, you will all see that I can also do it in numbers of other ways: there is no need to multiply examples.[9]

Moore claims that "the proof which I gave was a perfectly rigorous one; and . . . it is perhaps impossible to give a better or more rigorous proof of anything whatever."[10]

We can provide an equally "rigorous" proof of the existence of colored objects in much the same way. With my right hand I pick up an apple and say, as I make a certain gesture, "Here is a red apple." With my left I pick up another red apple and say, as I make a certain gesture, "And here is another." In doing this, I have, apparently, proved the existence of at least two red things and have thereby established that colors are exemplified by something. And this conclusion is incompatible with color skepticism.

Moore's confidence that his is a rigorous proof is based in part upon the fact that the conclusion follows strictly from the premises. In the corresponding proof about colors, the conclusion that there are colored objects follows strictly from the premises as well. An argument that succeeds in *proving* the truth of its conclusion is one that establishes that the conclusion is something that is *known* to be true. In order for the conclusion to be known, the premises must be known as well. One's rational confidence in the conclusion of an argument can be no greater than one's rational confidence in the premises. Moore claims that he knows the truth of the premises of his proof:

> I certainly did at the moment *know* that which I expressed by the combination of certain gestures with saying the words 'There is one hand and here is another.' . . . How absurd it would be to suggest that I did not know it, but only believed it, and that perhaps it was not the case! You might as well suggest that I do not know that I am now standing up and talking—that perhaps after all I'm not, and that it is not quite certain that I am.[11]

By analogy, again, one might present the case against color skepticism by insisting that one does *know* the premises of the corresponding argument. If one does know the truth of "Here is a red apple, and here is another," then color skepticism is clearly refuted.

Moore realized that many philosophers would be dissatisfied with his proof. He points out that they would not take his argument to be a proof of the external world unless he could also provide a proof of its premises. For the doubt about its conclusion can just as easily be transferred to its premises. The skeptic can reply to Moore that he does not really know the truth of the proposition expressed by "There is one hand and here is another." Moore concedes that he is unable to supply the desired proof. "How am I to prove now that 'Here's one hand, and here's another?' I do not believe I can do it." But this admission of inability to provide a proof does not show, says Moore, that he failed to prove the existence of the external world. For "I can know things, which I cannot prove; and among things which I certainly did know, even if (as I think) I could not prove them, were the premises of my two proofs."[12] Similarly, the counter–color skeptic may insist that even if he could not prove the truth of "Here is a red apple, and here is another," nevertheless, that is among the propositions that can be known without proof. One knows it by seeing the apples and seeing what colors they have. One simply makes use of the plain evidence of the senses.

Let M stand for Moore's proof about his hands and C for the corresponding proof about the red apples. M takes Moore's hands for its subject matter, but, as Moore points out, there are countless similar proofs of the external world that differ from M only in the choice of external objects that are used in their premises. Let A be a proof just like M, except that instead of having Moore's hands as its subject matter, it uses the very same apples mentioned in C. Whereas C ostensibly proves that colored things exist on the basis of the fact that certain colored apples exist, A purports to prove that external things exist on the basis of the fact that these apples exist. Just because the items that are taken to exemplify colors in C are also external objects, if C proves that colored objects exist, it follows that A proves that external objects exist. However, if A proves that external things exist, it does not follow that C proves that colored things exist. For the proposition, for example, that apples exist does not entail that apples of a certain color or, for that matter, of any color exist. So neither M nor A of itself constitutes an argument against color skepticism, even if they are successful, as Moore thinks, in refuting the Cartesian skeptic.

So if C is successful against color skepticism, its success cannot be fully explained by its logical similarity to A or to M. The main issue is whether one knows the premises of C as Moore claims to know the premises of M or could claim to know the premises of A. It is plausible to assert that the knowability of the premises of C

is no less than the knowability of the premises of *A*. For the way one establishes that here are two apples is by holding them up and looking at them; but one gets to know that here are two red apples in the very same way. So one who knows the premises of *A* is also in a position to know the premises of *C*.

However, the color skeptic can reply that the premises of *C* have a richer content than those of *A*. For "Here are two red apples" strictly entails "Something is red" and "Something is colored," whereas the premises of *A* have no such strict entailment. So it does not follow strictly from the fact that one is in a position to know that the external world exists, that one is also in a position to know that colors exist.

The color skeptic claims that although most people believe that there are colored things and most people would claim to know that there are colored things, there are no colored things and, therefore, nobody knows that there are. Our great confidence that there are is based upon an uncritical reliance upon the evidence of the senses. The color skeptic bases his argument in part upon certain premises drawn from empirical science that support the view that the theories that provide causal explanations of the occurrence of visual experience in animal organisms do not imply or presuppose the existence of colored objects. On the basis of such premises together with much philosophical argumentation (as presented in this book), the color skeptic asserts that nothing that we know or have any rational assurance of supports the claim that something colored exists. By appealing to contingent premises drawn from empirical science to deny the claim that anyone knows the truth of the premises of *C*, color skepticism presupposes the existence of an external world. So color skepticism is quite unlike Descartes's radical general skepticism based upon the dream and evil genius arguments. It is more like skepticism about the existence of phlogiston or the ether than it is like skepticism about the existence of the external world.

There is a certain type of argument that Moore used against skepticism that can be drawn upon to strengthen M. Perhaps it can also be used against the color skeptic. It goes like this. Skepticism about the external world, if it is reasonable, must itself be based upon an argument that has a skeptical conclusion (e.g., "I do not know that any external objects exist") that is supported by certain premises. Moore would claim that it is more certain that the premises of M or of A are true than that the skeptic's premises are true, whatever they are.[13] Similarly, the counter–color skeptic may reasonably assert in the course of holding aloft a red apple and making a certain gesture with it that he is more certain that this is red than he is certain of the premises of the arguments of the color skeptic.

Now, which premises does the counter-skeptic wish to reject as being insufficiently certain? The scientific argument originating in Locke that I have used to support color skepticism, when fully formulated to take into account the concepts and theories of contemporary color science,[14] relies on certain propositions of atomic physics, of optics, of chemistry, and of human physiology and biology. If we had to choose between accepting color skepticism and casting these aside, we would certainly accept color skepticism and retain our science. For casting aside the conclusions of color science would throw into doubt the ability of modern science to explain anything, whereas adopting color skepticism instead would leave our entire explanatory apparatus intact and would have no significant practical consequences.

However, not all the premises of color skepticism are scientific.

There is at least one that is epistemological. For we need some principle concerned with the fixation of belief that mediates the transition from the scientific facts and theories to the disbelief in color. Such a principle would say roughly that if a theory that explains why it perceptually appears as if there is a certain entity of kind K does not imply or presuppose that there are entities of kind K, then the fact that it perceptually appears that there are Ks is not a sufficient reason for believing that there are Ks. Let us call it *the principle for the ontological evaluation of perceptual appearance* (or "POPA" for short). It is a principle that is susceptible of wide and varied use. For example, it justifies us in saying to those who sincerely claim to have seen ghosts or demons or angels that they saw no such thing even though it seemed to them that they saw them. It justifies us in saying that it is reasonable to doubt the existence of colored objects despite the appearances to the contrary.

The counter-skeptic may decide to reject POPA as being less certain than the existence of colors. But how are we to judge certainty here? We could rely upon our common sense intuitions to guide our way. In that case we would cast color skepticism aside and perhaps POPA as well. But our common sense intuitions are not infallible. Sometimes *they* are worthy of being cast aside. Among the circumstances in which they should be cast aside is when they are unsupported by established and well-confirmed scientific results. But in order to make use of science to criticize and evaluate common sense, we need either POPA or a principle very much like it. In general, an epistemology that allows us to criticize the appearances is one that, when combined with science, will render color skepticism plausible. Counter-skepticism will lead us to give up more in the way of belief that is valuable than does skepticism.

Notes

CHAPTER ONE

1. John Locke, *An Essay Concerning Human Understanding*, ed. P. H. Nidditch (Oxford: Clarendon Press, 1975), IV, xxi, 4.
2. Galileo, "The Assayer," in *Discoveries and Opinions of Galileo*, trans. Stillman Drake (New York: Doubleday, 1957), p. 274.
3. Ibid., p. 238.
4. Thomas Hobbes, *The Elements of Law*, ed. Ferdinand Tönnies (Cambridge: Cambridge University Press, 1928), p. 7.
5. Ibid., p. 6. In *Leviathan*, (Oxford: Clarendon Press, 1967), chap. 1, p. 11, Hobbes replaces the theory of rebounds with a theory of endeavors. Perhaps the change is only verbal.
6. *Leviathan*, chap. 1, p. 12.
7. See the first objection in the third set of objections to Descartes's *Meditations* written by Hobbes. This is included in *The Philosophical Writings of Descartes* (Cambridge: Cambridge University Press, 1984), vol. II: 121.
8. Hobbes, *Elements of Law*, p. 7.

9. Ibid., pp. 3–4.
10. *Leviathan*, chap. 1, p. 12.
11. George Berkeley, *A Treatise Concerning the Principles of Human Knowledge* (New York: Liberal Arts Press, 1957), sec. 49, p. 46.

CHAPTER TWO

1. John Locke, *An Essay Concerning Human Understanding*, ed. P. H. Nidditch (Oxford: Clarendon Press, 1975), IV, iii, 16.
2. Ibid., II, xxi, 1–2.
3. Ibid., II, viii, 17.
4. Ibid., II, viii, 10.
5. Ibid., II, viii, 15.
6. Ibid., II, viii, 24.
7. Ibid., II, viii, 16. An earlier version of the same argument can be found in Descartes's *Meditations*. See *The Philosophical Writings of Descartes* (Cambridge: Cambridge University Press, 1984), vol. II: 57.
8. I am here taking the liberty of modernizing Locke's science.
9. In Locke, *Essay*, II, ix, we are given examples of how judgments influence and modify sensations.
10. In his "Epistemology Naturalized," W. V. Quine writes: "Epistemology, or something like it, simply falls into place as a chapter of psychology and hence of natural science. It studies a natural phenomenon, viz., a physical human subject" (*Ontological Relativity and Other Essays* [New York: Columbia University Press, 1969], p. 82). Except for the reductionist implication in the use of "physical," this is a good partial description of how Locke understood the enterprise of epistemology.

CHAPTER THREE

1. C. L. Hardin, *Color for Philosophers* (Indianapolis: Hackett, 1988), pp. 148–54. This book became available just as I was completing my final

revisions. Hardin makes use of the facts and theories of color science to criticize objectivist accounts of color. His own view is briefly expressed as follows: "We are to be eliminativists with respect to color as a property of objects, but reductivists with respect to color experiences" (p. 112). I am not sure whether or not his eliminativism cum reductivism entails what I have called color skepticism. In Chapter Six, I provide some reasons to be less optimistic regarding mind-body reductivism than is Hardin.

2. For Alfred North Whitehead, see *Process and Reality*, corrected edition (New York: Free Press, 1978), pp. 11–13.

3. See the discussion of counter-factuals in D. M. Armstrong, *What Is a Law of Nature?* (Cambridge: Cambridge University Press, 1983).

CHAPTER FOUR

1. John Locke, *An Essay Concerning Human Understanding*, ed. P. H. Nidditch (Oxford: Clarendon Press, 1975), II, viii, 19.

2. Thomas Reid, *Philosophical Works* (Edinburgh, 1895), vol. I: 318.

3. Ibid., p. 315.

4. Ibid. An earlier formulation of the microstate theory of secondary qualities is expressed in Hobbes's remark: "All which qualities called *Sensible,* are in the object that causeth them, but so many several motions of the matter, by which it presseth our organs diversely" (*Leviathan* [Oxford: Clarendon Press, 1967], chap. 1, pp. 11–12).

5. Reid, *Works*, I: 313.

6. Ibid., p. 258.

7. Ibid., p. 310.

8. Ibid., p. 312. It is not clear to me how one can render consistent the following four claims that Reid makes: that we are directly acquainted with the primary qualities of bodies, that sensations occur as signs of the items perceived, that sensations do not incorporate any conceptions, and that perception is not the effect of reasoning.

9. Ibid., p. 327.

10. Ibid., p. 319.

11. Here is how Bertrand Russell has made a similar point: "The particular shade of colour that I am seeing may have many things said about it —I may say that it is brown, that it is rather dark, and so on. But such statements, though they make me know truths *about* colour, do not make me know the colour itself any better than I did before: so far as concerns knowledge of the colour itself, as opposed to knowledge of truths about it, I know the colour perfectly and completely when I see it, and no further knowledge of it itself is even theoretically possible" (*Problems of Philosophy* [London: Oxford University Press, 1951], pp. 46–47).

12. The classic formulation of this point occurs in the first of George Berkeley's *Three Dialogues Between Hylas and Philonous*.

13. I am here trying to elucidate what our conceptions of visual perception and color are. Since I shall subsequently argue for color skepticism, my characterization of our conception of color should not be interpreted as endorsing the view that it corresponds to anything that actually occurs.

14. The qualification "for human beings in this world" is intended to allow for the possibility that we are born with innate knowledge of colors. That is a logical possibility that is not realized in the actual world.

15. Saul A. Kripke, "Naming and Necessity," in *Semantics of Natural Language*, ed. Donald Davidson and Gilbert Harman (Dordrecht, Holland: D. Reidel, 1972), pp. 353–54.

16. See C. L. Hardin, *Color for Philosophers* (Indianapolis: Hackett, 1988), pp. 7–19, for an extensive discussion.

17. See Hilary Putnam, "The Meaning of 'Meaning,'" in *Philosophical Papers* (Cambridge: Cambridge University Press, 1975), vol. II: 215–71, for arguments in support of this point.

18. See Russell, *Problems of Philosophy*, pp. 41–42.

CHAPTER FIVE

1. John Locke, *An Essay Concerning Human Understanding*, ed. P. H. Nidditch (Oxford: Clarendon Press, 1975), III, iii, 18.
2. Color television is a similar case. See C. L. Hardin's interesting discussion of it in *Color for Philosophers* (Indianapolis: Hackett, 1988), p. 72.
3. It may be more plausible to say not that colors do not exist, but that nothing exemplifies color. I will consider the difference between these two claims in Chapter Eight.

CHAPTER SIX

1. There are uses of "see" that do not entail existence, such as "He sees pink elephants." I do not think that too much should be made of such cases; occasionally "see" is used for the same purposes as "looks."
2. See T. L. Sprigge, "Consciousness," in *The Ontological Turn*, ed. M. S. Gram and E. D. Klemke (Iowa City: University of Iowa Press, 1974), pp. 114–47; and Thomas Nagel, "What Is It Like to Be a Bat?" in *Mortal Questions* (Cambridge: Cambridge University Press, 1979), pp. 165–80.
3. Sprigge, "Consciousness," p. 117.
4. Nagel, "What Is It Like?" p. 175.
5. Descartes, *Philosophical Letters*, trans. Anthony Kenny (Oxford: Clarendon Press, 1970), p. 103.
6. For a recent discussion of this hypothesis in which it is made a premise of a reductionist argument, see John Searle, *Minds, Brains and Science* (Cambridge: Harvard University Press, 1984), p. 19.
7. I take the reductionist claim to be a case of token-token identity. Even the materialistically inclined functionalist who claims that functional states are realized in the brain is committed to token-token identity as the only plausible interpretation of what 'realization in the brain' amounts to.

8. Spinoza, *Ethics*, part III, prop. 2, scholium, trans. James Shirley (Indianapolis: Hackett, 1982), pp. 105, 106.

9. For a defense of this position, see Richard Rorty, "Mind-Body Identity, Privacy, and Categories," *Review of Metaphysics* XIX (1965): 24–54.

10. Aristotle, *De Interpretatione*, 16a3–8, trans. J. L. Ackrill, in *The Complete Works of Aristotle*, ed. Jonathan Barnes (Princeton: Princeton University Press, 1984), vol. I: 25.

11. Thomas Hobbes, *Leviathan* (Oxford: Clarendon Press, 1967), chap. 4, p. 24.

12. John Locke, *An Essay Concerning Human Understanding*, ed. P. H. Nidditch (Oxford: Clarendon Press, 1975), III, ii, 1.

13. I borrow this term from Jerry A. Fodor, *The Language of Thought* (New York: Thomas Y. Crowell, 1975).

14. Franz Brentano, *Psychology from an Empirical Standpoint*, ed. Linda L. McAlister (New York: Humanities Press, 1973), pp. 88–89.

15. Brentano would not agree. Ibid., pp. 80, 198, 201.

16. For an excellent elaboration and defense of this view, see D. M. Armstrong, *Perception and the Physical World* (London: Routledge and Kegan Paul, 1961), chaps. 7 and 9.

17. John Searle, *Intentionality* (Cambridge: Cambridge University Press, 1983), p. 39.

18. Ibid.

19. Ibid.

20. Ibid., p. 40.

21. Ibid., p. 46.

22. Ibid.

23. This point was raised by Jerry Fodor and Jerry Katz in a discussion of a paper on which this chapter was based.

24. Fred Dretske, *Seeing and Knowing* (Chicago: University of Chicago Press, 1969), pp. 20–49, 78–93.

25. John Dewey in his essay "Qualitative Thought," reprinted in *On Experience, Nature and Freedom*, ed. Richard J. Bernstein (New York:

Liberal Arts Press, 1960), pp. 176–98, discusses features that pervade and unify perceptually presented situations.

26. Bertrand Russell, *Problems of Philosophy* (London: Oxford University Press, 1951), p. 135.

27. Searle, *Intentionality*, p. 52.

28. Aron Gurwitsch, "Husserl's Theory of the Intentionality of Consciousness," in *Husserl, Intentionality, and Cognitive Science*, ed. Hubert L. Dreyfus (Cambridge: MIT Press, 1982), p. 61.

29. Ibid., p. 64.

30. Ibid., p. 61.

31. Ibid., p. 63.

32. Searle, *Intentionality*, p. 51, and Ludwig Wittgenstein, *Philosophical Investigations* (Oxford: Basil Blackwell, 1953), part II, p. xi.

33. This was defended by Colin McGinn in a discussion.

CHAPTER SEVEN

1. C. J. Ducasse, *Nature, Mind, and Death* (LaSalle, Ill.: Open Court, 1951), p. 259.

2. Ibid., pp. 278–79.

3. C. L. Hardin, *Color for Philosophers* (Indianapolis: Hackett, 1988), p. 82.

4. Wilfrid Sellars, "Foundations for a Metaphysics of Pure Process," *Monist* LXIV (1981): 62.

5. Ibid., p. 68.

6. Ibid., p. 64.

7. H. H. Price, *Perception* (London: Methuen, 1954), p. 3.

8. It does not follow that there is no place for imaging.

9. The term "presentational immediacy" is Whitehead's. See, for example, his *Symbolism, Its Meaning and Effect*, in *Alfred North Whitehead: An Anthology*, ed. F. S. C. Northrop and Mason W. Gross (New York: Macmillan, 1953), p. 540.

CHAPTER EIGHT

1. For the facts of color science and their application to the issue of the ontology of color, see C. L. Hardin, *Color for Philosophers* (Indianapolis: Hackett, 1988), chaps. 1 and 2.
2. This point was made by Jerry Fodor in a conversation.
3. H. H. Price, "Appearing and Appearances," *American Philosophical Quarterly* I (1964): 16.
4. But see Hardin's argument against the simplicity of colors in *Color for Philosophers*, pp. 42–43.
5. C. A. Strong, "On the Nature of the Datum," in *Essays in Critical Realism*, ed. Durant Drake (New York: Peter Smith, 1941), pp. 241, 243. This book was first published in 1920.
6. W. V. Quine, *From a Logical Point of View* (New York: Harper and Row, 1963), p. 10.
7. Hilary Putnam, *Reason, Truth and History* (Cambridge: Cambridge University Press, 1981), p. 146.
8. This difficulty was pressed on me by Arthur Collins.
9. G. E. Moore, *Philosophical Papers* (New York: Crowell-Collier, 1962), p. 144.
10. Ibid.
11. Ibid., p. 145.
12. Ibid., p. 148.
13. Ibid., p. 222.
14. See Hardin, *Color for Philosophers*, chap. 1.

Index

Index

Index